# Target English Reading

GW00502987

Helen Lines

Bekah Mardall

www.harcourt.co.uk

✓ Free online support
✓ Useful weblinks
✓ 24 hour online ordering

01865 888080

Heinemann

Heinemann is an imprint of Harcourt Education Limited, a company incorporated in England and Wales, having its registered office: Halley Court, Jordan Hill, Oxford OX2 8EJ. Registered company number: 3099304

www.harcourt.co.uk

Heinemann is the registered trademark of Harcourt Education Limited

Text © Harcourt Education 2007

First published 2007

12 11 10 09 08 07

10 9 8 7 6 5 4 3 2 1

British Library Cataloguing in Publication Data is available from the British Library on request.

ISBN 978 0 435118 60 0

Designed and Typeset by Kamae Design

Original illustrations © Harcourt Education Limited 2007

Illustrated by Kathy Baxendale, Chris Brown, Leo Brown, Paco Cavero, Janos Jantner, Gillian Martin, Andy Morris, Sam Thompson, Mark Turner and Rory Walker

Cover design by Zannah Hawdon

Picture research by Caitlin Swain

Cover photo © Photodisc / SuperStock

Printed by Printer Trento

Acknowledgements

The author and publisher would like to thank the following individuals and organisations for permission to reproduce photographs:

POPPERFOTO/Alamy pp4/5; Corbis pp6/7/68 (top) /82 (left); Alt-6/Alamy p8; F. S. Westmorland/Science Photo Library pp16/17; The Film Works Ltd p21; Terry Fincher.Photo Int / Alamy p24; Dale O'Dell / Alamy pp26/27; Bill Bachmann / Alamy pp26/27; Ronald Grant Archive pp34/35/74/76/114/119; COURTESY OF LUCASFILM LTD. Copyright and Trademark Notice: Star Wars Episode III – Revenge of the Sith © 2005 Lucasfilm Ltd. & ™. All rights reserved. Used under authorization. Unauthorized duplication is a violation of applicable law pp36/37; photos.com p44/45 (centre); NASA pp45 (bottom)/47 (top) /48/49; PhotoDisc. StockTreck pp46/47 (centre) 48–53; Getty Images / PhotoDisc pp56/57/78/79; istockPhoto. Jose Fuente pp 58/59/71; Ralph A. Clevenger/ CORBIS pp60/61/72; Digital Vision p62; Robert Fried / Alamy pp64/65; Julie Mowbray / Alamy p66; Harcourt Education Ltd. Debbie Rowe p68 (right and left); Galen Rowell / Mountain Light / Alamy p70; Getty Images / John Lund p73; PhotoDisc / Photolink pp82/83 (middle); Denis Hallinan / Alamy p85; Icon/Ladd Co/Paramount/ Kobal Collection pp 92/93; iStockPhoto / Richard Stanley pp100/103; Creatas pp104/105/106; The Print Collector / Alamy p108 (top); Getty Images p108 (bottom); Columbia/Marvel / The Kobal Collection pp116/117; Alex Cunningham / Alamy pp122/123; Tony Watson / Alamy pp124/125.

Every effort has been made to contact copyright holders of material reproduced in this book. Any omissions will be rectified in subsequent printings if notice is given to the publishers.

Player quotes are used with kind permission from the National Literacy Trust reading promotion DVD Reading the Game – The Movie. The DVD was produced by Lion TV with support from the Professional Footballers' Association and the Department for Education and Skills. Live footage of players is provided by the Football Association; 'Jabberwocky' by Lewis Carroll 1832–1898; Extract and front cover from The Iron Man by Ted Hughes, published by Faber and Faber. Reprinted with permission of Faber and Faber Limited; Extract from Max Fax: Sharks by Claire Llewellyn, published by Hodder & Stoughton. Reprinted with permission of Hodder and Stoughton Limited; Extracts from The Loch Ness Project www.lochnessproject.com. Reprinted with kind permission; Loch Ness Monster eyewitness account by Mrs Moir, found on www.nessie.co.uk; Extract from www.intotheblue.co.uk. Reprinted with permission of Activity Gift Vouchers Ltd; Quotes from the motion picture Star Wars: Episode III – Revenge of the Sith. © Lucasfilm Limited & ™. All right reserved. Used under authorization; Extract from The War of the Worlds by H. G. Wells. Reprinted with permission of A P Watt Ltd on behalf of the Literary Executors of the Estate of H. G. Wells; Extract from Speedy Reads: Moon Landing. Text copyright © Nick Arnold, 2001. Reproduced with permission of Scholastic Ltd. All rights reserved; Extract from Exodus by Julie Bertagna, published by Young Picador, 2003. Reprinted with permission of David Higham Associates Limited; Use of the book cover from Life of Pi by Yann Mantel, published by Canongate Books. Reprinted with permission; Extract from www.gobroadreach.com. Reprinted with permission of Broadreach Summer Adventures for Teenagers.

# Contents

# why read?

Why do people read?

What do they like reading?

> I read the papers every day and keep up with what's happening in the world. I read the football magazines to relax and a lot of autobiographies.

> I like reading about stuff that's real, biographies about people and books about real things. And my favourite book as a kid was *The Twits* by Roald Dahl.

> When you read books like *The Hobbit*, you can escape. It's a classic and one of the best books out there.

from the DVD *Reading the Game*, produced by the National Literacy Trust in 2006

4

Reading is a good way of finding out about the world around you.

## Ask yourself

What Kind of Reader Am I? Create a picture of you as a reader.

Put your name, or a picture of yourself, in the middle of the sheet. Next, cut out the statements that describe you as a reader and stick them onto the sheet. The closer to the centre of the sheet, the more they apply to you. When you have finished, compare your reading profile with a friend's. Remember, all readers are different.

Take your completed poster to your next English lesson and stick it into your exercise book.

I read quickly.

I talk about books with other people.

I read slowly.

I sometimes feel happy or sad when I read.

I skip boring parts.

I picture the places, the people and events in the books I read.

I read aloud.

I read in bed.

I read silently.

I prefer silence when I read.

I read alone.

I can often predict what will happen in a story.

I prefer reading while listening to music.

I prefer stories to information books.

I read with other people.

I prefer information books to stories.

I get easily distracted when I read.

I stop reading if I don't like a book.

I often get 'lost' in a book.

I always finish a book whether I like it or not.

I could never read a book more than once.

I often look at the ending when I am in the middle of reading a book.

I think about books after I've finished reading them.

I often re-read my favourite books.

I never look at the end of the book when I am in the middle of reading it.

# This is your brain

The left side of your brain controls your logical thinking and language skills.

## You are learning:

How to be an active reader who searches for meaning

- It weighs about 1.3 kg – a bit more than a bag of sugar.

- It makes up 2% of your body weight.

- It's 75% water.

- It's about 140mm wide, 167mm long and 93mm high – go on, measure it!

- It contains about 15 billion cells.

- About 750ml of blood pumps through it every minute.

- It gives out enough energy to power a 10-watt light bulb.

- It can generate more ideas than the number of atoms in the entire universe.

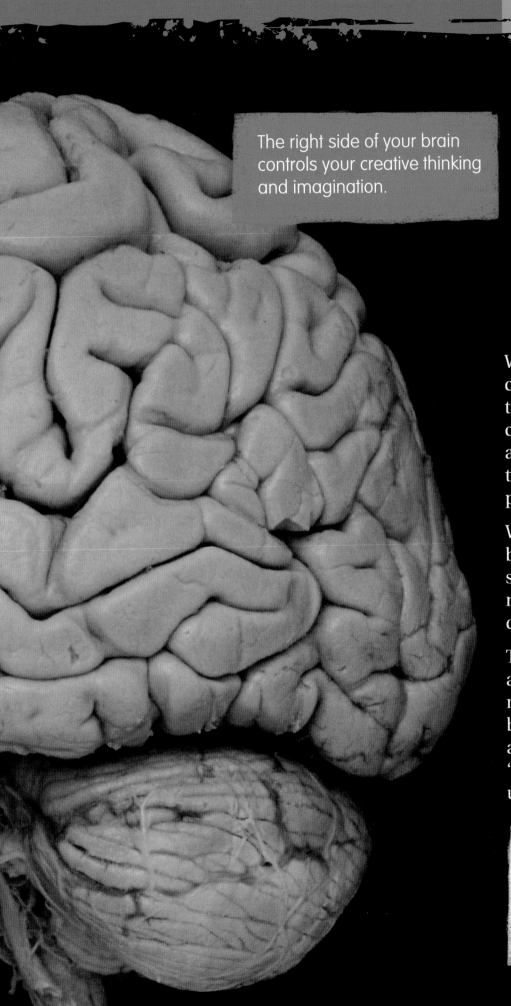

The right side of your brain controls your creative thinking and imagination.

When we think, brain cells from both sides of the brain send electrical charges to each other, a bit like electricity travelling down wires to power a searchlight.

When we read, we use brain cells from both sides of the brain to make connections that create meaning.

To get better at reading, and to enjoy reading the most, we need to use both sides of the brain and switch on all the 'searchlights' that help us make meaning.

## Ask yourself

What does your brain have to do with your reading?

7

# How to be an active reader

Reading is an active search for meaning. When we use our brain to read, we …

→ … use our knowledge of grammar to help us make sense of the text. We look for patterns in the way language is used and how the text is organised.

## You are learning:
How to be an active reader who searches for meaning

→ …. use clues about context to help us make meaning. We link the text to things we already know or can predict, and we pick up clues from pictures or the layout of the text.

→ … recognise how words look and know how they sound. We use our graphic knowledge and phonic skills to help us decode the text.

**Use clues about how words look and how they sound to read for meaning in unfamiliar texts.**

What to do when you come across unfamiliar words:

- pick out key words in the text that you already know by sight, to help you understand what the text is about.

- look for letter chains that you know, especially at the start of a word, e.g. ch-, st-, br- and at the end of a word, e.g. -ing, -ed, -tion.

- chunk the word into syllables and say each syllable.

- say each different phoneme in the word and then blend them together, e.g. b/r/i/dge; sh/ou/t; ch/ur/ch.

- does it look or sound like other words you know? See if the new word fits a familiar pattern or rhyme, e.g. *knight* is like *fight, fright* and *bright*.

- use your best guess then read the word again. Does it look right and sound right? Does it make sense in the sentence?

 **Use knowledge of grammar to read for meaning in unfamiliar texts.**

- Read from the beginning of the sentence again then look at the unfamiliar word. What would fit best and make sense?

- Read ahead to the end of the sentence and then go back to the unfamiliar word. What would fit best and make sense?

- What does the word do in the sentence? Use grammar clues to help you recognise or 'best guess' an unfamiliar word, e.g.

  - a noun that has *the* or *a* in front of it or a noun with a capital letter that names a person or a place: *Mr Harris, Switzerland.*

  - an adverb ending in *-ly* that tells you more about an action: *The dog growled menacingly.*

  - an action verb that ends in *-ing* or *-ed*: We were *suffering* in the heat. We *staggered* on.

- Look for punctuation that will help you read the sentence and understand what it means, e.g. full stops, question marks and speech marks.

**Use context clues to read for meaning in unfamiliar texts.**

- What kind of text is this? Where would you find it? Who is it for?

- What would you expect to find in this kind of text?

- Link the unfamiliar text to similar ones that you've seen or read before, to help you make sense of it and predict what might happen.

- If there are pictures in the text, what information do they give you? Can you make links between the pictures and the words?

- Re-read the parts before and after the unfamiliar word to remind yourself what the text is about. What word would make sense? Does the word actually say that?

- If you think you've misread a word, stop and check it again. Self-correct it whenever you can.

# Monsters in fiction: 'Jabberwocky'

## You are learning:
How to use context clues to read for meaning

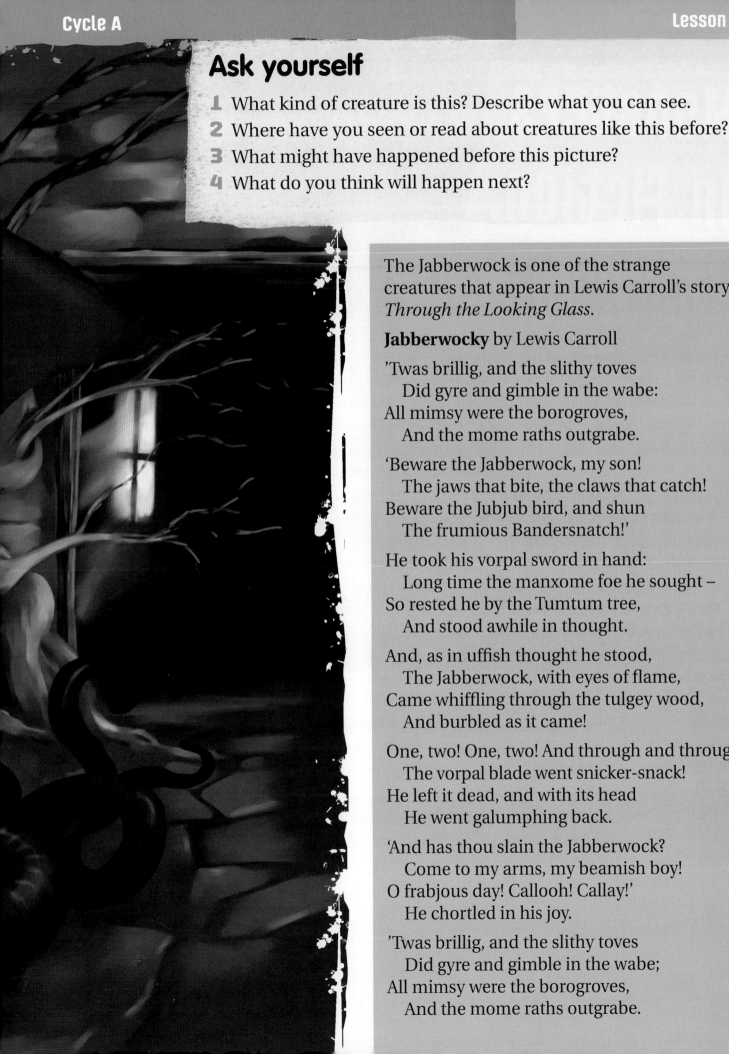

## Ask yourself

1 What kind of creature is this? Describe what you can see.
2 Where have you seen or read about creatures like this before?
3 What might have happened before this picture?
4 What do you think will happen next?

The Jabberwock is one of the strange creatures that appear in Lewis Carroll's story, *Through the Looking Glass*.

**Jabberwocky** by Lewis Carroll

'Twas brillig, and the slithy toves
  Did gyre and gimble in the wabe:
All mimsy were the borogroves,
  And the mome raths outgrabe.

'Beware the Jabberwock, my son!
  The jaws that bite, the claws that catch!
Beware the Jubjub bird, and shun
  The frumious Bandersnatch!'

He took his vorpal sword in hand:
  Long time the manxome foe he sought –
So rested he by the Tumtum tree,
  And stood awhile in thought.

And, as in uffish thought he stood,
  The Jabberwock, with eyes of flame,
Came whiffling through the tulgey wood,
  And burbled as it came!

One, two! One, two! And through and through
  The vorpal blade went snicker-snack!
He left it dead, and with its head
  He went galumphing back.

'And has thou slain the Jabberwock?
  Come to my arms, my beamish boy!
O frabjous day! Callooh! Callay!'
  He chortled in his joy.

'Twas brillig, and the slithy toves
  Did gyre and gimble in the wabe;
All mimsy were the borogroves,
  And the mome raths outgrabe.

# Monsters in Fiction: The Iron Man

## You are learning:
How to use context clues to read for meaning

At the start of this story by Ted Hughes, a huge giant made out of metal suddenly appears in England. At first, people are afraid of him, but by the end of the story he is a hero who saves the Earth from a terrible monster: the Space-Bat-Angel-Dragon.

## Ask yourself

1 How can you tell that this is the front cover of a fiction book?

2 Does this front cover make you want to read the story? Give reasons for your answer.

3 What do you think will happen in the story?

4 Do you think the Iron Man is a good character or a bad character? Give your reasons.

Taller than a house, the Iron Man stood at the top of the cliff, on the very brink, in the darkness. The wind sang through his iron fingers. His great iron head, shaped like a dustbin but as big as a bedroom, slowly turned to the right, slowly turned to the left. His iron ears turned, this way, that way. He was hearing the sea. His eyes, like headlamps, glowed white, then red, then infrared, searching the sea. Never before had the Iron Man seen the sea.

from *The Iron Man* by Ted Hughes

r CHILDREN'S CLASSICS

ff

THE IRON MAN

Ted Hughes

## Assess your progress

You have been using context clues to read for meaning.

Look again at the information about using context clues on page 9.

Which clues have you found the most useful?

# Monsters of the deep

When you come across a word you don't know:

- look closely at all parts of the word.

- break the word down into syllables.

- sound out the word.

- read the sentence again.

- read to the end of the sentence, then go back to the hard word.

- think about what you expect the text to say and see if it fits with what's on the page.

- ask yourself if what you have just read sounds right and makes sense.

- think whether this text is like other things you have read.

- see if there are any other clues to help you, such as illustrations and headings.

- if you are not sure what the writer is telling you, go back and read again.

## Blue whale

- At 30 metres long, the blue whale is the biggest animal that has ever lived on Earth.

- It breathes through two blowholes and sounds as loud as a jet plane.

- The blue whale lives near the surface of the ocean, on its own or in a small group called a pod.

- It eats krill, small fish and plankton and gets through 4 million krill a day.

# Giant octopus

- The giant octopus is about 9 metres long and weighs 45 kilograms.
- It has four pairs of arms which are about 5 metres long.
- The giant octopus is usually browny-red but it can change colour to blend in with its surroundings.
- Its arms are lined with suckers that can hold onto prey or other objects.

# Giant white shark

- The great white shark can swim as fast as 60 kph.
- An adult shark is 12 metres long and can weigh as much as 2000 kilograms.
- Its teeth are 6 centimetres long and it uses them to bite and tear its prey.
- Its skin is as rough as sandpaper.
- Great white sharks may attack humans but they do not eat them.

# Giant squid

- The giant squid lives 900 metres down in the depths of the sea.
- It has a thick body and long, thin tentacles.
- At about 15 metres, the giant squid is longer than a London bus.
- Its body does not have any bones.
- It squirts black ink at its enemies.
- Sightings of live giant squid are very rare.

## Ask yourself

These huge sea creatures really are monsters of the deep. But which one is which? Match the right fact card with the right monster.

# The facts about sharks

**You are learning:**
How to use reading strategies to search for meaning

Be an active reader who searches the text to find out what it means:

- SKIM the text to find out what it's about and who it's for.

  Run your eyes quickly over the text, from left to right and up and down. Look at titles and headings, words in bold type, and illustrations. Cover the text. What do you remember seeing? What was in the top left corner? The bottom right corner? The centre? Uncover the text and see if you were right.

- SCAN the text to look for facts and answers.

  Move your eyes from left to right, right to left, working down the text. Look for names with capital letters, numbers, and key words. What three things can you remember?

- ASK QUESTIONS to help you read the text more closely.

  Search for answers to 5W questions: Who? What? Where? When? Why?

The shark is the king of the sea. It is fast and fierce. It fills people with fear. But that's not the whole story. Yes, some kinds of shark are dangerous, but most of them are harmless and shy.

There are more than 350 kinds of shark in the sea, and they come in many shapes and sizes. The Pygmy shark could lie in the palm of your hand. The Whale shark is longer than a bus.

Sharks spend their lives in water. They have the perfect body for the sea. It is smooth, strong and shaped like a torpedo. It is driven by a powerful tail.

A shark's eyes never close. When it is about to attack, a thin piece of skin slides over the eyes to give them extra protection. Sharks' skin feels rough. It is covered with small, thorny scales called denticles.

A shark's teeth are triangular, and point backwards towards the throat. They have pointed tips and serrated edges, and cut just like a saw.

from *Sharks* by Claire Lewellyn

## Assess your progress

- Can you explain how you skim and scan a text?

- Can you make up some 5W questions about sharks using this text?

# The story of Beowulf and Grendel

Practise using reading strategies by looking carefully at the film poster and answering the questions about it.

Using knowledge of grammar to read for meaning:

- Which words did you read first? Why?
- How can you tell that Beowulf and Grendel are the names of the main characters in the story? Do you think they are friends or enemies?
- Find the sentence that sums up the story. What does it tell you?

This is a poster that advertises a film.

Using context clues to read for meaning:

- What is the title of the film?
- Who are the stars of the film?
- Describe what you can see on the poster.
- What do you think will happen in the film?
- Do you think you would like this film?

Using graphic and phonic clues to read for meaning:

- Which words on the poster do you recognise straight away?
- Which words are harder to read? What is hard about them?
- What strategies can you use to help you read the difficult words?

## Ask yourself

Were these questions easy to answer? Which ones were the hardest and why?

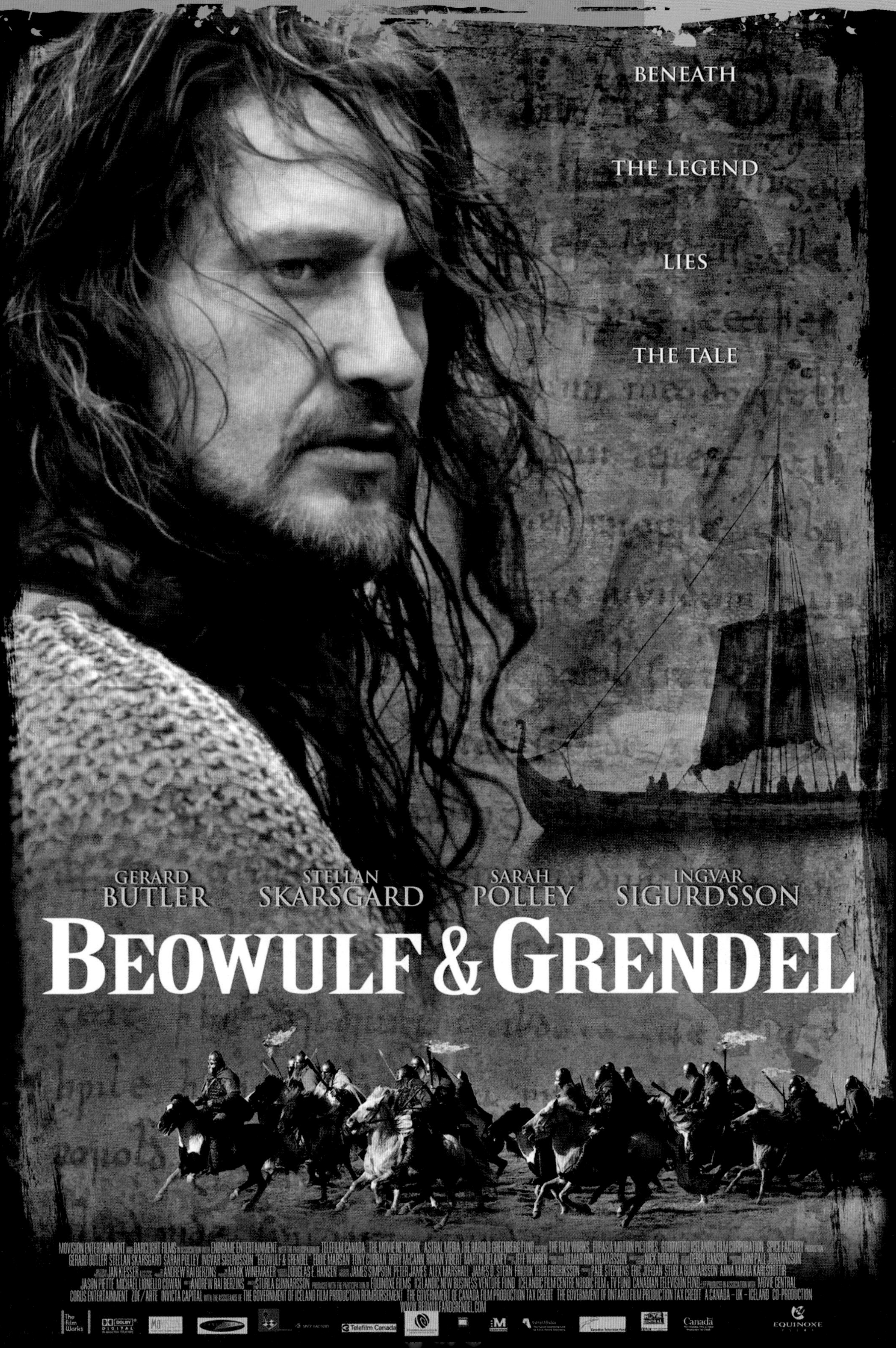

BENEATH

THE LEGEND

LIES

THE TALE

GERARD
BUTLER

STELLAN
SKARSGARD

SARAH
POLLEY

INGVAR
SIGURDSSON

# BEOWULF & GRENDEL

# Beowulf and Grendel

The story of Beowulf and Grendel was told over a thousand years ago.

The people of Denmark were threatened by a bloodthirsty monster called Grendel, who killed and ate humans. The king of Denmark, Hrothgar, asked the mighty Swedish warrior Beowulf to help him catch and defeat Grendel. In a final battle at Hrothgar's hall, Beowulf ripped off Grendel's arm and the monster fled in agony to die alone.

4

## Ask yourself

Look carefully at the
storyboard and the stills
from the film, *Beowulf and
Grendel*. Active readers
search for meaning by:

**Visualising:**
- What can you see?
- What do you imagine?

**Asking questions:**
- WHO is in the story?
- WHAT is happening?
- WHERE does it take place?
- WHEN does it happen?
- WHY does it happen?

**Predicting and speculating:**
- What has happened before?
- What might happen next?
- What clues make you think this?

# Beowulf and Grendel's final battle

## You are learning:

How to be an active reader who searches for meaning

**5**

Here is the story leading up to Grendel's final battle with Beowulf:

From the misty hills of the lonely moor, Grendel came stalking, striding through the night, into the hall where the warriors slept. In a rage, his eyes like fire, that terrible creature hurried to Hrothgar's hall, hungry for blood and bones. When he touched the heavy door with his hands, it gave way at once. Quickly the beast moved across the mead hall floor. He saw the warriors sleeping, stretched out snoring, all but one of them. For Beowulf stood in the shadows, ready to strike.

Grendel reached out his mighty arm and hooked a warrior into his mouth. He bit into the bones, drinking the streams of blood and swallowing huge mouthfuls of flesh. Quickly he ate that man, down to his hands and feet. Then he reached for Beowulf.

But Beowulf struck fast. He grasped at Grendel's arm and gripped it hard, clinging to it until the fingers broke. Then the bones gave way and the monster's arm snapped loose. Howling in pain, he dragged himself to the door of the hall and fled into the dark night, back to the lonely moor. His life had reached its end.

In Hrothgar's hall, Beowulf lifted Grendel's huge and heavy arm for all to see. The warriors stared in wonder. Grendel's death made no one sad.

## Assess your progress

In this cycle of lessons you have been an active reader who searches for meaning. Use a traffic light rating system to assess how confident you feel about using each of the reading strategies that are listed below. Green = I can do this easily; amber = I still need some help with this; red = I need lots of help with this.

| Reading strategy | Rate yourself |
| --- | --- |
| Using grammar and context clues to help you understand what an unfamiliar word means (knowing what kind of word it is and what type of text it comes from) | |
| Using graphic and phonic clues to help you understand what an unfamiliar word means (knowing what the word looks like and sounds like) | |
| Visualising (using what you see and imagine to help you understand the text) | |
| Asking 5W questions (who, what, where, when and why) to help you understand the text | |
| Predicting and speculating to help you understand the text (thinking about what might have happened before and what might happen next) | |

# The Loch Ness Monster: fact or fiction?

**You are learning:**
How to find information in non-fiction texts

There have been many reports of sightings of the Loch Ness Monster, but how can you decide whether to believe them?

**Where does the monster live?**

Dores

Drumnadrochit

*Loch Ness
Exibition Centre*

Foyers

Invermoriston

*Loch Ness*

Inverness

Fort William

Fort Augustus

## Facts about Loch Ness

Loch Ness is the largest of three lochs (lakes) which run for over 60 miles from Inverness in the north to Fort William in the south. During the last ice age, which ended about 12 000 years ago, the whole area was covered in 4000 feet of ice. It was this ice that carved out the trough that Loch Ness lies in.

There is more water in Loch Ness than in all the other lakes in England, Scotland and Wales put together. It is 22 miles long and 1.5 miles wide. It has a depth of 754 feet, and the bottom of the loch is as flat as a bowling green. It could hold the population of the world ten times over.

Because of the great amount of water in the loch, it never freezes. Apart from the top 100 feet of water, the temperature stays at 44 degrees Farenheit, so as the surface water cools in the winter and nears freezing point, it sinks and is replaced by warmer water from below. This can cause the loch to steam on very cold days. In fact, in winter the loch gives off as much heat as would be produced by burning 2 million tons of coal.

## Ask yourself

**Skim** the text about Loch Ness: run your eyes down the centre and read a few words either side of this central line. This will give you a general idea of the facts about Loch Ness.

**Scan** the text about Loch Ness: pick out the names of places (look for nouns with capital letters) and figures (look for numbers).

Use the information to answer the questions below.

1 Where is Loch Ness?
2 When was Loch Ness formed?
3 How long, how wide and how deep is Loch Ness?
4 What is unusual about the bottom of Loch Ness?
5 Why does Loch Ness never freeze?

## What does the Loch Ness Monster look like?

Many people claim to have taken photographs of the Loch Ness Monster, but are they genuine?

## Assess your progress

In this cycle of lessons, you are using different reading strategies independently to find information in non-fiction texts. You are:

- skimming and scanning
- asking questions
- using punctuation clues to read ahead
- selecting details
- re-reading to check information
- recording details.

Check your progress as an active reader who searches for information. Describe:

- Two things you know you can do well.
- One thing you know you can improve.

## Ask yourself

What is similar about these photographs? What is different about them?

Draw one animal based on the information shown in all the pictures.

**Who has seen the
Loch Ness Monster?**

**9** In May 1933 Mrs Mackay said she saw something resembling a whale. 'It was huge and had a humped back.'

**8** On 30th July 1979, also at Temple Pier, Alistair and Sue Boyd parked in a lay-by at about 4.15 p.m. They first saw 'a small object moving into the bay but then a huge hump rose to the surface. It was about the size of a yacht hull.' By the time they had found their camera, the creature had disappeared.

**7** In 1900 John McLeod was fishing from a rocky ledge above a pool in the river. He saw a creature that had 'a head like an eel and a long tail.' He cast his line in its direction and it moved away.

**6** In 1934 Alex Campbell saw 'a long-necked creature' near Fort Augustus. He said it looked like a plesiosaur, an animal that lived before the dinosaurs and was believed to be extinct.

**Invermoriston**

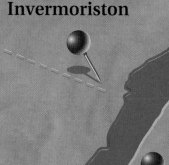

**Fort Augustus**

**1**

In AD 565 Saint Columba saw a 'water monster' attack a man. The man was swimming across the River Ness to collect a boat from the other side when the beast attacked him. Saint Columba formed the sign of the cross and shouted at the monster to go back. It quickly disappeared.

Dores

**2**

In August 1963 Hugh Ayton was working in his garden one evening when he saw something out on the loch. He launched a boat and set out after it. Mr Ayton saw 'a neck about 6 feet long, a head like a horse and humps above the water. The skin looked rough and there was an eye looking at me.' Then the creature dived and did not appear again.

nadrochit

**3**

On 22nd July 1933 Mr Spicer and his wife were driving along the south shore, when at about 3.30 p.m. they saw something crossing the road. Mr Spicer said, 'It was the closest thing to a dragon or prehistoric animal that I have ever seen in my life. The creature had a long neck and looked like a dinosaur.'

Foyers

**4**

On 12th November 1933 Hugh Grey was walking by the loch when he saw something 'very great' in the water. He did not see the head but noticed that the tail was thrashing about in the water. He took five photographs, one of which became the first known monster photograph. Some people have suggested that one shows a Labrador dog with a stick in its mouth.

**5**

On 28th February 1960 at Horseshoe Scree, Mr Torquil MacLeod saw a huge animal half out of the water. 'It had a pair of paddles and something like an elephant's trunk in front,' which Mr MacLeod thought was the neck. After a few moments, it flopped into the water and went straight down.

## Ask yourself

List all the details that describe what the Loch Ness Monster looks like, according to these eyewitness accounts. What are the similarities? What are the differences?

Whose story do you most believe and why?

29

# Who has seen the Loch Ness Monster?

**You are learning:**
How to retrieve information from non-fiction texts

Read the following account of a sighting of the Loch Ness Monster made by Mrs Moir of Inverness in October 1936.

One October afternoon a friend took my sister, mother-in-law, my young daughter and myself for a little trip by car to Foyers. On the return journey, at a place where the road runs very close to the Loch, about three miles from Foyers, my sister suddenly shouted, 'Look, there's the Monster'.

We all got out of the car and ran to the water's edge. There, before us, at a distance of a third of the width of the Loch away from us, was this wonderful creature. It was a perfect view. If we'd had a camera, it would have been the most convincing picture of the Monster ever taken, but alas! we had neither camera nor binoculars.

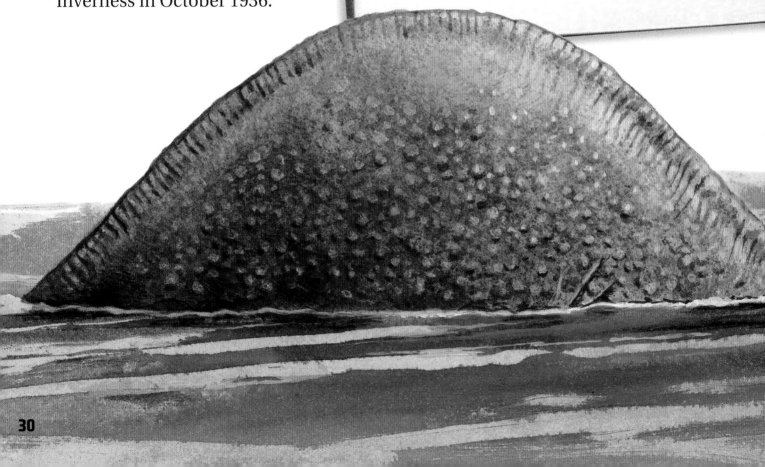

There were three humps, a long slender neck ending in a small head, and the overall length appeared to be about 30 feet. I could see no details of eyes or mouth but the outline was all beautifully clear – the three humps, head and neck. The middle hump was the highest, the one behind the neck was smaller, and the in-between size was at the back, sloping in a graceful line down to, and under, the water. The creature often dipped its head into the water either feeding or amusing itself.

We watched in awe and amazement, for over 5 minutes, then it suddenly swung round away from the shore, and shot across the Loch at a terrific speed, putting up a wash. When it eventually came to rest, I noticed the humps had disappeared; the back was now more or less straightened out, but the neck and head were as before.

The creature was in full view for 15 minutes. I have no idea how much of the body was underneath the water, but what we saw was a huge creature, very powerful, graceful and quite at ease in the water. A thrilling experience – I actually saw the Loch Ness Monster, resting, and travelling at speed.

## Ask yourself

Which details in Mrs Moir's account do you think are the most convincing and realistic?

Which details made it hard to believe her story?

# A monster from Greek myth: the Minotaur

## You are learning:

How to retrieve information from fiction texts

## Ask yourself

Describe the Minotaur and its surroundings in as much detail as you can. Then, bearing this information in mind, say why it would be hard for Theseus (and Ariadne) to kill the Minotaur.

## Theseus and the Minotaur

A long time ago, on the island of Crete, King Minos ruled his people through force and fear. To amuse himself, he built a palace with a deep cellar beneath it, full of twisting tunnels and dead ends. At the very centre of this labyrinth he kept a terrible monster, the Minotaur, who was always hungry for human flesh. Every year King Minos threatened his neighbours, 'Unless you send me seven juicy young men and seven young and tender women to feed my beast, I'll sink your ships and make war on you.'

One year, Prince Theseus of Athens said to his father, King Aegeus, 'This madness has to stop. This year I'll go as one of the fourteen chosen ones and I will kill the Minotaur!' And nothing the king could say would change his mind.

At the entrance to the labyrinth, Theseus felt his courage draining away. Deep in the darkness he heard the Minotaur, half man, half bull, stamping and snorting, its hoofs and horns scraping the walls of the maze.

Then Theseus felt a ball of string pushed into his hand. Ariadne, King Minos' daughter, was deeply ashamed of her father's cruelty and determined to end it. Now she whispered, 'Here, Theseus, take this. Tie one end around this stone pillar and unwind the string as you go. Then you can find your way back out of the labyrinth.'

Theseus inched forward into the darkness. Suddenly the Minotaur was crashing towards him, bellowing loudly. One bony horn caught Theseus' arm and gashed it open, but Theseus fought back strongly. He darted around the monster, flicking the loose end of the string into its face, and diving out of sight beneath its belly, until he had sent the beast half mad with frustration. Once the Minotaur was distracted, Theseus leapt onto its back and grabbed one of its horns, forcing the creature's head backwards. He drew back his arm and plunged his dagger hard into the Minotaur's neck. The great beast shuddered and roared with pain, then slowly sank to the cold stone floor, defeated.

## Assess your progress

In this cycle of lessons, you have been using reading strategies independently to understand and retrieve information from fiction and non-fiction texts. Give yourself a 1–3 star rating for each of the skills listed below. 3 stars = I can do this easily; 2 stars = I can do this with some help; 1 star = I need a lot of help with this.

- Use different strategies to read unfamiliar words, e.g. phonic knowledge, grammar and context clues.
- Scan text to locate specific details.
- Identify and select the main ideas in texts.
- Usually notice when something I read doesn't make sense and try reading it again.
- Read ahead to make sense of the whole sentence.
- Understand straightforward facts and ideas in texts.
- Recount main events or facts with some help.
- Express an opinion or preference.
- Find some details in the text in answer to specific questions.

# Alien worlds

What do you imagine when you think of worlds beyond the Earth? This is how some famous films have imagined them.

## You are learning:

How to read for meaning and support ideas with evidence from the text

### Plot outline:
A group of Earth children help a stranded alien to return home.
(*E.T.*)

### Plot outline:
A computer hacker learns from mysterious rebels about the true nature of his reality and his role in the war against the controllers of it.
(*The Matrix*)

### Plot outline:
A group of people witness UFOs flying through the night sky. Meanwhile, government officials discover physical evidence of alien visitors. Both groups must follow clues to experience a close encounter of the third kind – contact.
(*Close Encounters.*)

### Plot outline:
A mining ship, investigating a suspected SOS, lands on a distant planet. The crew discover some strange creatures and investigate.
(*Alien*)

## Ask yourself

Can you match each plot outline to the right film picture?
What do these stories of alien worlds have in common?

# Imagine another world ...

1 EXT. SPACE

A long time ago in a galaxy far, far away ...

A vast sea of stars serves as the backdrop for the Main Title, followed by a ROLLUP, which crawls into infinity.

War! The Republic is crumbling under attacks by the ruthless Sith Lord, Count Dooku. There are heroes on both sides. Evil is everywhere.

In a stunning move, the fiendish droid leader, General Grievous, has swept into the Republic capital and kidnapped Chancellor Palpatine, leader of the Galactic Senate.

As the Separatist Droid Army attempts to flee the besieged capital with their valuable hostage, two Jedi Knights lead a desperate mission to rescue the captive Chancellor.

PAN DOWN to reveal a REPUBLIC ATTACK CRUISER. Continue to PAN with the Cruiser as TWO JEDI STARFIGHTERS enter and head towards an enemy Battle Cruiser. TRACK with the Jedi Fighters as they manoeuvre in unison, dodging flack and enemy laser fire. R2-D2 is on Anakin Skywalker's ship. R4-P17 is on Obi-Wan Kenobi's ship. A giant space battle is revealed as the tiny Jedi ships continue their assault in a synchronous ballet.

2 INT. OBI-WAN KENOBI'S STARFIGHTER COCKPIT – SPACE

OBI-WAN KENOBI bounces through the flack with a frown. His ship rocks violently.

3 INT. ANAKIN SKYWALKER'S STARFIGHTER COCKPIT – SPACE

ANAKIN SKYWALKER smiles as he blasts a TRADE FEDERATION DROID DROP FIGHTER.

ANAKIN SKYWALKER: There isn't a droid made that can outfly you, Master, and no other way to get to the Chancellor ...

OBI-WAN KENOBI: Look out, four droids inbound ...

- Have I seen anything like this before?
- Where would I expect to see images like this one?

- When I look at this image, what do I see first?
- What details do I notice when I look more closely?

- When I look at this image, what else do I want to find out?
- What 5W questions would it be useful to ask? (Who, What, Where, When, Why)

- When I look at this image, what does it make me think of?
- How does it make me feel?

## Assess your progress

You have been using the following strategies to help you read and think about images connected with 'alien worlds': visualising, empathising, asking questions, predicting and speculating. Which ones did you find most helpful?

Can you think of any other lessons where you can use them to help you read and understand images?

## Ask yourself

Can you carry on the script opposite? What might happen next? What would you see on the screen? What would you hear on the soundtrack?

# Do aliens exist?

## You are learning:

How to read for meaning and support ideas with evidence from the text

For years, we Earthlings have wondered whether we are alone in the universe or whether we've got company in the shape of aliens. People claim to have met aliens and seen UFOs – unidentified flying objects – and some people even say they've been abducted by extra-terrestrials. But what do we really know about them – do they exist at all?

Is there any evidence of life on other planets? Use the information that follows to help you make up your mind.

SIGN IN    CHAT    VOTE    SEARCH

 HOME

 NEWS

 PHOTO GALLERY

CONTACT US

## DO ALIENS EXIST ...

For years, people have speculated about whether life could exist outside Earth.
Now we want to know what you think!

Do you believe E.T. really exists?

Or do you think it's all a load of rubbish, made up by people with over-active imaginations?

Or do you agree with some scientists who think that alien life form exists, but in the form of tiny organisms rather then little green Martians.

Add your comments now or click on the voting button above to have your say!

## Ask yourself

Look in the text for answers to these 5W questions:
- Who has seen evidence that aliens exist?
- What might aliens look like?
- When have aliens been spotted?
- Where could aliens be from?
- Why is it hard to be sure if aliens really exist?

# DO YOU BELIEVE IN ALIENS

### Who has seen evidence that aliens exist?

Thousands of people are convinced that aliens have visited Earth. But no-one has ever actually reported finding an alien 'in the flesh'. There are lots of photos and films of apparent sightings of alien spacecraft but most of these can be explained. They are probably low-flying planes, part of an army or air force exercise, or weather balloons. And of course some 'photographs' of aliens and spacecraft have turned out to be fakes.

### What might aliens look like?

We don't really know what aliens would look like. Are they really little green men or huge scary monsters, like in some movies? Do they have eyes on stalks or two heads? According to experts, if aliens do exist they are more likely to be small and look like worms or other bugs.

### When have aliens been spotted?

One of the most famous 'sightings' of aliens was in New Mexico, USA. On 8 July 1947, the army said they'd found a 'flying disc' which had crashed onto a ranch in Roswell. Much later, people found out that it was only an instrument for measuring changes in the weather.

In 1989, a doctor who had worked at Roswell claimed that bodies of aliens had been found and autopsies carried out on them but this also turned out to be untrue – they were dummies used by the army to fire at.

### Where could aliens be from?

All life as we know it needs water to survive. Because of this, scientists think that Mars is the most likely planet in our solar system to have aliens living on it, as it contains water. However, it's likely that these 'Martians' would live underground as the surface of Mars is thought to be too harsh for life to exist.

### Why is it hard to be sure if aliens really exist?

We have only just begun to explore space. The universe could contain thousands of solar systems which haven't yet been discovered. This means that there may be lots of other planets capable of supporting life. So, even if aliens are never found in our solar system, it's very possible that there's life on planets that has yet to be discovered.

# What are we doing to find aliens?

Do aliens exist? Have your say.

'I think, out of the trillions of stars in our universe and hundreds of planets orbiting them, the chances of there being life elsewhere are extremely high. On Europa (one of Jupiter's moons), the huge ocean under the sheet of ice could be a perfect habitat. Also the phrase 'little green men' could be so wrong. They could look exactly like us.'

**Ben, 12, Southampton**

'I think there is life on other planets, but people in this world shouldn't be spending ridiculous amounts of money on expeditions into space when the money could be going to help people in poverty in this world! What is the point in looking for life on other planets when we can't even get our own planet sorted out!!'

**Carmel, 15, Glossop**

'When you consider the size of the universe I believe it's hard to imagine that we really are the only form of life around. I think there is definitely life on other planets, and perhaps in our own Solar System, it's just that it might take decades to find it.'

**Kathryn, 15, Dundee**

## Ask yourself

- Which of these views do you most agree with, and why?

- How would you answer the question: Do aliens exist?

# War of the Worlds

## You are learning:

How to read for meaning and support ideas with evidence from the text

*The War of the Worlds* is one of the most famous science fiction stories of all time. The original was written by H.G. Wells in 1898. It told the story of Martians attacking England with their deadly Tripod fighting machines and a Heat Ray that burnt everything in its path.

In 1938, the story was broadcast in America as a radio play. It was so realistic that two million listeners in New Jersey thought they were being attacked by aliens from Mars! Since then, different versions of the story have been published as comics and as films.

In this extract from *The War of the Worlds*, a spaceship from Mars, shaped like a big cylinder, lands in the south of England. The cylinder begins to open, and the narrator describes seeing a Martian for the first time.

## Ask yourself

From these images, what do you think happens in the story of *The War of the Worlds*?

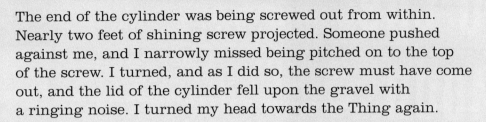

The end of the cylinder was being screwed out from within. Nearly two feet of shining screw projected. Someone pushed against me, and I narrowly missed being pitched on to the top of the screw. I turned, and as I did so, the screw must have come out, and the lid of the cylinder fell upon the gravel with a ringing noise. I turned my head towards the Thing again.

I think everyone expected to see something like a man emerge – I know I did. But, looking, I presently saw something stirring within the shadow. Something resembling a little grey snake, about the thickness of a walking stick, coiled up out of the middle of the cylinder and wriggled in the air towards me – and then came another, and another, each with two luminous discs like eyes.

A sudden chill came over me. There was a loud shriek from a woman behind. I half turned, still keeping my eyes fixed on the cylinder, from which more tentacles were now projecting. Those who have never seen a living Martian cannot imagine the strange horror of their appearance. A big greyish, rounded bulk the size of a bear was rising slowly and painfully out of the cylinder. As it bulged up and caught the light, it glistened like wet leather. Two large dark-coloured eyes were staring at me. It was round and had, one might say, a face. There was a peculiar V-shaped mouth under the eyes, with a pointed upper lip. The mouth quivered and panted, and dropped saliva. The body heaved and pulsated. One lank tentacle gripped the edge of the cylinder, another swayed in the air. Terror gripped me. I stood petrified and staring…

## Ask yourself

- Is this what you expected a Martian to look like?
- Which details do you most remember, and why?

## Assess your progress

You have been learning to support your ideas with evidence from the text. How confidently can you find details in a text that help you answer specific questions?

# To the Moon

**You are learning:**

How to make judgements about texts and support your ideas with evidence

What is the Moon like? Is it made of cheese? Does it really cause 'lunacy' or madness? Is there a man in the Moon? Is it unlucky to look at a new Moon through a window? People have been fascinated by the Moon for centuries, but on 20 July 1969 we found out what the Moon was really like when American astronauts set foot on it for the first time.

- When you look at this image, what more do you want to find out?
- Is there anything that puzzles or interests you?
- What 5W questions would help you find out more about this event? (Who, What, Where, When, Why)

- What is the most striking thing about this image?
- What details do you notice when you look more closely?
- Can you see any patterns or contrasts?
- What words and phrases can you use to describe what you see?

- What is this person thinking and feeling?
- Would you want to be in this person's shoes and do what they are doing?
- Would you like to meet this person?
- If you met this person, what questions would you want to ask them?

## Ask yourself

Use the questions on these pages to help you look closely at the photographs and respond to them. Record your answers to the questions and compare them with a partner's.

When Neil Armstrong first set foot on the Moon he said, 'One small step for a man. One giant leap for mankind.' What do you think he meant?

- Have you seen anything like this image before?
- What do you already know about this topic?
- What might a photograph taken before this one show?
- What might happen next?

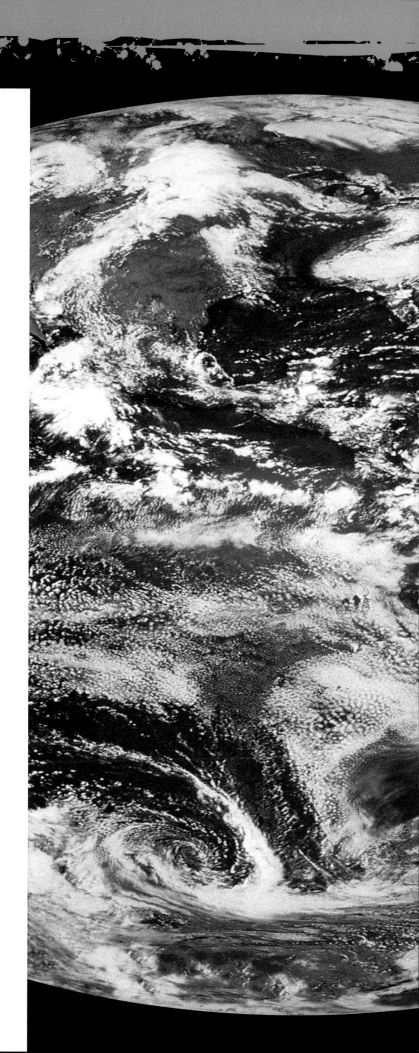

### Thursday 16 July 1969
### 9.27 a.m.: Lift-off

At the launch site in Houston, the mission controller wishes the astronauts a happy flight. Four minutes later the computer takes over the launch sequence. The countdown begins:

'10, 9, 8 …' White-hot fingers of flame reach out from the rocket. Thousands of litres of cooling water spray the launch pad. A mist of super-hot steam and fire roars around the *Saturn V*.

'7, 6, 5 …'

Blankets of smoke roll into the air.

'4, 3, 2 …'

The ground begins to shake.

'1, ZERO!'

'Lift-off – we have lift-off!'

The blast is awesome. The rocket rises slowly, battling against its own vast weight. As it burns up fuel, it lightens and then rises faster and faster into the morning sky.

The crowd gasps. 'GO! GO! GO!' they yell. Some people are crying.

Through the window, the astronauts see the Earth's shining blue oceans and restless clouds. They unbuckle their safety belts and feel their bodies lifting off their seats. Carefully, they remove their helmets and gloves, which then hover silently in the air. They're weightless!

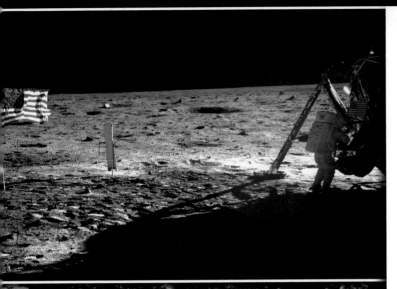

### Monday 20 July: Lift-off + 102 hours, 45 minutes: Moon landing

You can slice the air at mission control with a razor. Hundreds of eyes are glued to flickering computer screens. There's no sound. No one dares move.

Finally the voice of Buzz Aldrin crackles from the loudspeaker: 'OK, engine stop … command override, off; engine arm, off. 413 is in.'

Then they hear Neil Armstrong's voice: 'Houston, this is Tranquillity base. The *Eagle* has landed.'

The astronauts help each other with their packs and check the tubes that connect the packs with the space suits. And now – at last – Houston says, 'GO!'

### Monday 20 July: Lift-off + 109 hours, 19 minutes: One small step

Armstrong backs out of the *Eagle* spacecraft on his hands and knees and begins to clamber down the ladder. He's desperately excited, but struggles to hide it. His body feels light, but clumsy.

Armstrong glances down and tells Houston what he sees. 'The surface appears to be very, very fine grained … it's almost like a powder,' he reports. His voice is electric with tension.

He switches on a camera. Back on Earth, one-fifth of the world's population is watching every move on TV. Where it's night-time on Earth, children are woken up to witness the greatest moment in scientific history.

Neil grips the rungs as he carefully descends the metal ladder. Every nerve is tingling. 'I'm going to step off … now!' he says.

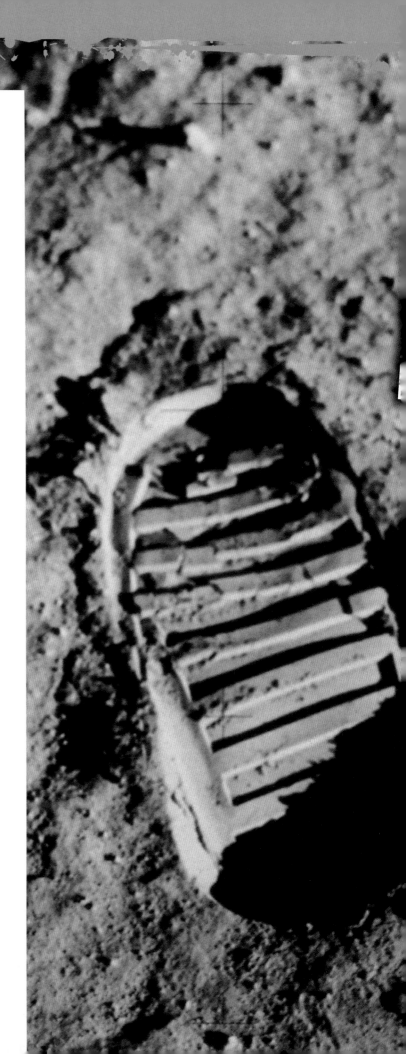

He carefully lowers his right boot on to the dusty surface. He says the words that will go down in history: 'One small step for a man. One giant leap for mankind.'

Neil grinds his boot into thick dust. It's like black powdered charcoal. He can see the clear rounded print of his boot on the ground. Then he scoops up a dirt sample and hops slowly around the *Eagle*, looking for damage. There's none. Moving feels strange – like running in slow motion.

Neil takes pictures using a camera strapped to his chest. He snaps Buzz descending the ladder. At the base of the ladder, the two men gaze at one another and glimpse their reflections in the golden visors of their space helmets. Then they unpack equipment for two experiments before hopping back to the *Eagle* to unveil a plaque: 'Here men from the planet Earth first set foot on the Moon, July 1969.' Next, they plant a United States flag in the dust.

There's no time to think. Neil scoops dust from the Moon and Buzz hammers tubes into the ground to collect samples. They haul the rocks back into the *Eagle* using pulleys. Armstrong flings away his used equipment and it flies off in slow motion. Finally, the astronauts climb the ladder and close the hatch. They've been on the Moon almost two and a half hours.

Outside, the Moon looks like a beach after a public holiday. There are footprints everywhere, a flag, and lots of litter. Neil realises that the Moon hasn't changed in hundreds of thousands of years. He imagines returning a million years from now and finding things exactly the same. Without wind or rain even their footprints might still be there. The rubbish left over from the mission will also be there. It can't be returned to Earth because the *Eagle* needs to be as light as possible in order to blast off from the Moon.

### Tuesday 21 July: Lift-off + 122 hours

'You're cleared for take-off,' says Mission Control.

The engine fires! The blast wave flattens the American flag and raises a cloud of Moon dust. The *Eagle* rises up from the Moon where it's been on the surface for less than one Earth day.

The astronauts push the precious samples - 22 kg of Moon rocks - into the *Eagle*. The jettisoned landing craft drifts off into space where it will float for ever. Then the astronauts plot the course for home. The Earth sweeps over the Moon's cratered horizon like a small blue and white marble … and now at last they're going home!

# Moon Landing

> ## You are learning:
> How to make judgements about texts and support your ideas with evidence

## Ask yourself

Look back at the text on pages 46–49 to find answers to these empathy questions:

1 When the rocket blasted off from Earth, how did the crowd react? Look for three things they did.

2 When the *Eagle* spacecraft landed on the Moon, how was everyone at mission control in Houston feeling? Quote the words that tell you.

3 When Neil Armstrong first backed out of the *Eagle* and climbed down the ladder onto the Moon, what was he feeling? Which words tell you?

4 List all the things the astronauts left behind them on the Moon. Do you think they should have left all these things?

5 Re-read the last part of the text, from 'The astronauts push the precious samples – 22 kg of Moon rocks – into the Eagle …' to the end.

   a Why does the writer use the word 'precious' to describe the samples of Moon rocks?

   b Why does the writer say the Earth is like 'a small blue and white marble'?

## Assess your progress

In the last cycle of lessons you have been learning to make judgements about texts and to support your views with evidence. Rate yourself on how confident you feel about these skills, using the table below.

| | |
|---|---|
| I can look closely at an image and think about what it means | Very confident<br>Quite confident<br>Not confident |
| I can read a text closely and visualise what is happening | Very confident<br>Quite confident<br>Not confident |
| I can read a text closely and empathise with what the characters are feeling and thinking | Very confident<br>Quite confident<br>Not confident |
| I can give my opinion about events, ideas or characters | Very confident<br>Quite confident<br>Not confident |
| I can find some details in the text in answer to specific questions | Very confident<br>Quite confident<br>Not confident |

# Science fiction

Across the gulf of space, minds that were vast and cool and unsympathetic, regarded this earth with envious eyes, and slowly and surely the Martians drew their plans against us. And invisible to us because it was so remote and small, flying swiftly and steadily towards us across that incredible distance, drawing nearer every minute by so many thousands of miles, came the Thing they were sending us, the Thing that was to bring so much struggle and calamity and death to the earth.

From *The War of the Worlds* by HG Wells

Is there life on other planets that we haven't yet discovered? Is time travel possible? What will the world be like in 2500? These are just some of the questions that might inspire people who write science fiction. The short extracts on this page are from three different science-fiction stories. Read them and decide:

- What is the main idea about the future in each extract?
- Which story would you most want to read and why?

Mara's parents gaze in astonishment at the vast structure that rises out of the ocean – a giant city in the sky. The towers of New Mungo grow out of a central trunk, while massive roots bore down through the seabed, deep into the Earth.

Coll reaches out and squeezes Mara's hand.

'If this New World really is an option, then we need to figure out how to get to it – before we run out of time.'

From *Exodus* by Julie Bertagna

'Emergency! Emergency! We need urgent help!'

The Mission Control radio burst into life. All spaceships in this corner of the Solar System were listening.

'This is the *Argosy 9211*, on our way to Solar Station Three. Engines have failed! Life support is failing!
We are drifting towards the sun. Send help, please!'

From *Too Close to the Sun* by Andy Russell

# Ask yourself

Use the questions below to help you respond to these texts and make judgements about them.

- When you read this text, what do you 'see' or imagine?
- Which words and phrases create the strongest images for you?

- When you read this text, which bits do you like most?
- Which ideas do you most easily understand?
- Is there anything in the text that you dislike or ideas that you don't understand?
- Can you understand what the characters in the text are doing and thinking? Would you want to be in their shoes?

- What do you already know about this topic that might help you understand the text?
- Have you come across a story like this before?
- What do you think might happen in this story and what are the clues that tell you?

- When you read this text, what more do you want to find out?
- Is there anything that puzzles or interests you?
- What 5W questions would it be useful to ask to find out more about events and characters? (Who, What, Where, When, Why)

Now read these longer extracts, from *Exodus* by Julie Bertagna. In this story, global warming has caused the sea level to rise. Mara and her family go to New Mungo, a giant city built on the sea bed and reaching up into the sky. However, the city is already overcrowded and new arrivals are left to die in their boats outside its gates. In this part of the story, Mara steals a police uniform and slips into the city.

The door of the lift capsule to the sky city is wide open. Workers from the early morning supply ship are surging through, sweaty and dirty and tired, along with a squad of sea police. Wearing the orange uniform, it's easy to merge in. As she approaches the lift capsule she almost stops. A single step more will take her across the threshold that separates the two worlds. In the end it's the crush of those behind rather than her own will that pushes her through the doorway into the large golden capsule.

The next thing Mara sees when she steps out of the lift capsule is a line of city guards. Heart pounding, she avoids eye contact and walks past … Mara's stomach lurches, and not just from nerves. She feels as if she is on a ship at sea – gently but unnervingly the city sways to the rhythm of the world's wind, as  it is built to do.

'Hey, you! Over here' a guard shouts and Mara forces herself not to turn around but to keep moving with the rest. Her instinct is right. It's someone else they want. Mara follows the crowd from the supply ship down a short corridor and waits her turn in the queue, trying to look at ease but concentrating fiercely on everything around her.

'To enter, please insert your identi-disk here,' announces a voice, over and over, at the head of the queue. Its owner is a blankly smiling young woman who stands at the head of the corridor at what must be the official doorway to New Mungo … With relief, Mara sees that she's only a lumen-being, crafted from light … The lumen girl points at the slit in the wall where Mara should insert an identi-disk.

 'To enter, please insert your identi-disk here,' the lumen girl instructs.

Mara guesses and inserts one of the disks …

'Incorrect disk.'

The slot in the wall ejects the first disk … Mara doesn't dare look at the line of city guards and frantically, her fingers shaking, she inserts the second disk … The sliding door opens. Mara slips through, her heart beating painfully.

And is in! Amazed, she stands inside a long silver tunnel.

Mara wants to find the computer controls for New Mungo's high-powered boats. The plan is to escape in them to Greenland, which the sea has not yet covered. But before that, she needs to explore the city and find out how things work.

All she needs to do is to look as if she has lived in a sky city all her life – not easy when at every step there are such wonders that all she wants to do is stop and stare. Mara explores the city centre, trying to get her bearings …

Zoominium, says a sign above one large window. Mara peers through and sees what looks like a deep pool, but instead of water, people wheel and tumble through cascades of colour … Mara feels overwhelmed by so much glare, noise and movement, and by so many people.

But New Mungo is beautiful. Its long silver tunnels gleam and its arcades are vast airy places that look as if they, like the population of lumens, are crafted purely from light. The citizens are beautiful too … a world full of brilliant beings, human angels …

A happy crowd of boys and girls near her own age zip past on skates. So that's the secret of their speed and power! Mara stares enviously at their strong bodies, bright smiles and smooth skins. She stops at a humpbacked bridge that sits under a crystal sky and leans upon the bridge wall to look into the still mirror of a pond … Mara relaxes into the gentle wind-sway of the city as she watches the fish swimming round the Looking Pond and listens to the birdsong in the tree beside the bridge … A radiant sunset spreads across the screen of water, deepening and darkening until the pond is midnight black and full of star fire.

It would be so easy to forget the rest of the world, so tempting to slip inside this magic spell and ignore what lies outside …

Now the horror of the boat camp on the other side of the wall rushes upon her, along with the memory of her lost family. She looks at the pond with clear eyes. The fish are fake and swim in endless electronic circles. The tree and its bird, the crystal sky and sunset, are all fake too … It's a false enchantment.

## Assess your progress

You have been using reading strategies independently to make judgements about texts, supporting your ideas with evidence. Give yourself a star rating for each of the skills listed below: 3 stars = I can do this easily; 2 stars = I can do this with some help; 1 star = I need a lot of help with this.

- Identify and understand the main ideas in texts.
- Read a text closely and empathise with what the characters are feeling and thinking.
- Find some details in the text in answer to specific questions.
- Quote from, or refer to the text, to support my ideas with evidence.
- Give my opinion about events, ideas or characters.

# Be relevant!

## You are learning:

How to link details in order to make a deduction

The information you choose from a text or image must **fit** the statement that has been made about the text.

1. I must *go back* to the statement that has been made.
2. I must *remind myself* of the statement.
3. I must *check* the information I have found against the statement.
4. I must *decide* whether or not the evidence **fits** the statement.

**1**

These people are climbing over steep, rocky surfaces.

## Ask yourself

Who are these people and what are they doing?

**2** These people are well prepared.

**3** It is very cold.

## Making a deduction

The next step is to try to link up your ideas about a text and come to an answer, like a detective. We call this making a **deduction**.

- What are the links between the images in the circles and the information in the text?
- What can you work out about the whole picture by making links between the smaller parts?

# Be a detective: Make a deduction

## You are learning:

How to link details in a text in order to make a deduction

Now that you have learned to link up your ideas about an image, you can try to make some links between the information you can find in a text and **make a deduction**.

There are many dangers

The climbers are tired

My legs were heavy with the effort of the climb and my chest hurt when I breathed but it was time to move already. Luka had slumped down in the snow, breathing hard. The wind was like a bully. It pushed at our arms, our backs, our legs. The ledge we were standing on was narrow with steep drops all around. Even though our gloves were made of thick material, I could not feel my fingers. It was important for us to keep moving our feet and hands. I turned to Luka and made the signal to descend but got no response. Above our heads, clouds were forming. Soon we would not be able to see. I tried again, this time taking hold of Luka's arm. I shouted that it was time to go but he shook his head. Hooking my arm under his, I tried to take his weight but I was too weak. Breathing hard, I turned away and began the slow downward climb. I dug the spikes of my boots into the ice wall. I hoped that Luka was following me.

The weather conditions are getting worse

The air is extremely cold

## Ask yourself

What happened when the climbers reached the top of the mountain?

Use this sum to help you add the details together to form a deduction:

_____ + _____ = _____

# The icebers of meanins

**You are learning:**

That some meaning is hidden beneath the surface of a text

Icebergs are bigger than they appear: only a small part shows above the waterline. Most lies below.

Meaning is like an iceberg.

Some meanings are easy to find. These are on the surface of the text and we call them **literal** meanings.

Some meanings are more hidden and lie beneath the surface of the text. We call these **non-literal** meanings.

**Literal meaning**

- Things that the text tells me
- Things that are on the surface of the text

**Non-literal meaning**

- Ideas that the text suggests to me
- Ideas that are beneath the surface of the text

## Ask yourself

1 When I read a text, what information do I know for certain?

2 If I look beneath the surface of the text, what more can I find?

# what does it mean?

## Ask yourself

Which of these statements are literal statements?

Which statements are non-literal?

**You are learning:**
How to link details in order to make a deduction

→ This is a picture of a lion.

 This creature is powerful.

 The lion's coat is golden in colour.

→ The lion is resting.

 The lion is planning a hunt.

→ The lion is afraid.

 The lion is dreaming of meat.

→ This person is in danger.

→ This person is not in England.

The air was so hot that my skin was wet and my hair was stuck to my head. The map lay crumpled at my feet. My breathing was out of control. Flies buzzed in my ears, buzzed in my eyes, buzzed and buzzed around my mouth. A huge spider with a blood-red body waited in its web just above my head. I had always been afraid of spiders and now I was lost in a place where they crawled in their hundreds. My legs hurt from bending low to the ground for so long but I didn't dare to move.

→ The weather is hot.

A long, pink tongue licked a set of claws in lazy strokes. But those claws were sharp. Behind that soft tongue were rows of teeth as pointed as knives. The brightest orange eyes were turned towards me from across the stream. They had not looked away from me for ten long minutes. Terror bubbled in my chest. If I moved, he would be over the rocks and water in seconds and I would be ...I would be ...well, in a flick of his strong tail I feared I would be dead. And so I continued to wait, my camera heavy on my chest, my heart in my throat.

→ The creature is strong.

→ This person is being watched.

→ This person is feeling panic.

## Ask yourself

Now that you have read details in the text, it is time to put some of those details together and make a deduction: *What is this person doing?*

# Between the lines

## You are learning:
How to draw conclusions about meaning

It was important to move as slowly as possible.

A drum beat loudly.

He was determined.

His younger brother followed his lead.

## Assess your progress

- Can I ask questions that help me to dig beneath the surface of a text?
- Can I use different ways of reading to help me read beneath the surface of a text?
- Can I make a deduction based on details in the text?

## Ask yourself

How might these boys be feeling?

'Keep low. Keep low.'

The stories his grandfather had told him ran through his mind.

This was such an

# Skimming a text for meaning

The woman is wearing gloves

There are many steep surfaces in this place

There is a narrow pathway visible in the distance

This is a natural setting

## You are learning:

How to quickly work out what a text is about

Where have you heard the word 'skim' before?

Spend one minute thinking about the times and places you have heard or seen the word 'skim' and then share your ideas with a partner.

In this lesson you are going to learn how to 'skim' a text. What do you think this might mean?

When we skim a text, we look quickly through it so that we can skim off the overall meaning of the text and know what the whole text is about. Sometimes this is called 'getting the gist' of a text.

So, when we skim:

- we use our eyes
- we glance quickly through
- we focus on the main points
- we avoid being drawn into detail.

## Ask yourself

Which of these statements is a main point about the overall image?

Which of these statements is a detail of the image?

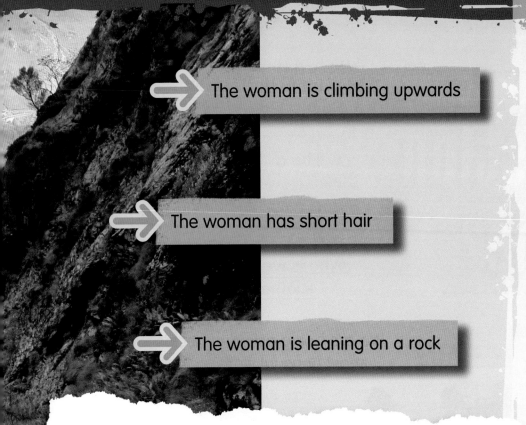

The woman is climbing upwards

The woman has short hair

The woman is leaning on a rock

So, to skim a text:

**1** I use my eyes to quickly skim for topic sentences or sub-headings in the text.

**2** I quickly read the topic sentences.

**3** I take a step back and make links between the topic sentences.

**4** I can put my understanding of what the whole text is about into words.

Gail was first reported missing at 2.34 p.m. She had been climbing alone on the cliffs above camp before lunch but had failed to return. The team knew Gail as a strong climber who had never been late back from a climb before. Very quickly her team mates grew worried.

After ten minutes the search party was ready and set off up the track. One member of the team carried the first aid kit in a rucksack; others carried water and energy bars. Two of the party carried the folded emergency stretcher, in case Gail had been injured.

Just before nightfall, a local herdsman gave directions into the hills beyond. The old man had seen a female climber walking in an easterly direction during the morning. He warned that the track was worn away and that footholds were not to be trusted. As the temperature dropped, the team pressed on up the valley.

Finally, only minutes before 10 p.m., a cry was heard in the distance. The team leader shone a powerful torch in the direction of the shout, which came from the base of a steep, rocky cliff face. Gail was discovered crouched over a broken ankle. Within minutes, the team had her fastened safely into the rescue stretcher and a satellite telephone call had been made, calling for a rescue helicopter.

## Ask yourself

When might it be useful to be able to skim a text?

# what is this question asking me?

Which of these bits of information is relevant to the question?

The answer will be a person.

The question is asking us to look at clothing.

We are looking for unusual clothing.

**Who** is wearing the **most** **unusual** **clothes** in these pictures?

We are being asked to decide which is the most unusual clothing in the pictures.

**You are learning:**
How to find the information you need

Is *this* detail relevant to the question?
Try to explain your answer.
So:

- read the question and decide what it is asking
- underline the key words of the question
- read the image for details that are relevant to the key words.

## Using topic sentences to map a way through a text

Topic sentences can help us to map our way through a text.
In this extract, the topic sentences are highlighted.

That strange evening in December, Sasha arrived home later than usual. He had chatted to friends outside the school gates and ridden his bike around the park with Owen. As he turned the key in the front door lock, he realised that his mum might be worried about him being late. The hands of the hallway clock showed that it was half past five.

The first time he heard it, Sasha was making his way down the long hallway to the kitchen. THONK! It sounded like wood hitting wood, a strange hollow sound which reminded Sasha of playing cricket in the summer.

'Mum! I'm home!' Sasha called up the stairs. The whole house was dark. There was only the yellow light from the street lamp shining through the diamond of glass in the front door to guide Sasha's hand as he felt for the light switch.

Sasha was starving as usual and headed for the snack cupboard, the first on the left in the kitchen. He was looking for the chocolate bar he had stashed so that his dad wouldn't find it. So it wasn't until he had ripped open the wrapper with his teeth, taking a satisfying bite of the chewy caramel and wafer, that he noticed the note on the table. It was written in slanted, hurried letters which he recognised as his mother's:

'Sasha, Bit of an emergency. Don't worry. Won't be long. Don't eat too many snacks - Aunty L is coming for dinner. Don't open the door of upstairs bathroom. Will explain when I get back. Mum x.'

Of course, Sasha headed straight for the stairs, taking them two at a time. As he lurched onto the landing he heard the strange sound for the second time: THONK! It was coming from behind the closed door of the bathroom. Slowing down, Sasha pressed his ear against the smooth wood of the door. THONK! He leapt back in shock and made a little squeal. Something behind the door, something quite large, moved.

Sasha headed for his bedroom, scooping his mobile out of his trouser pocket. He texted Owen: 'what's BIG and goes THONK? Think fast and txt me back. S.' Meanwhile Sasha ran through the possibilities in his own mind and tried to resist going back out to listen at the bathroom door.

It was another half an hour before Sasha heard a key in the front door lock and his mum's call up the stairs, 'Sasha, you back?' Sasha rushed to the top of the stairs and peered down to see his mother wrestling with a huge woven basket. His dad smiled. 'Guess what we've got in the bathroom?'

- When did Sasha arrive home?
- What was in the kitchen when Sasha arrived home?
- When he was in his bedroom, who did Sasha text?
- What happened after Sasha climbed the stairs?
- At what time did his parents finally arrive?
- Where did Sasha first hear the strange noise?

## Ask yourself

Can you use the detail in a paragraph to answer one of the questions?

- I can choose which paragraph to look more closely at.
- I can scan through that paragraph looking for a detail that answers the question.
- I can choose a detail in answer to the question.
- I can check the detail I choose by looking back at the question.

**69**

# Scanning a text for information

Skim this image. What is this image about?

## You are learning:

How to look for particular information in a text

When we first meet a text we might skim it. When skimming, we try to get an idea of what the whole text is about.

Scanning is different. When we scan we look closely for particular details.

Can you scan successfully?
- I use my finger to focus my attention.
- I move my attention from left to right.
- I keep reminding myself of what I am scanning for.
- I scan quickly but I don't rush.
- I check information I find against the question or statement.

Scan the image. Is this mountaineer using special equipment?

**Cally McGuinn was attempting to reach the summit of Mount Everest, the world's highest mountain. Sadly, that did not happen.**

Cally had climbed to Camp 4 on the South Col, waiting for the weather to break. As soon at the cloud and snow cleared she could try to reach the summit. The South Col lies at 7900 metres, which is about one kilometre below the summit of the mountain. This area of the mountain is known to climbers as the 'Death Zone' because oxygen levels are so low that the human body cannot survive there for more than a few days. Everest is so high that it pokes into the very cold high-speed winds of the Jet Stream. This can make camping conditions at Camp 4 miserable and dangerous, as Cally found out.

'I am writing this diary entry from Everest Base Camp, having returned late last night from the South Col. I was aiming to climb to the summit but unfortunately I didn't reach my goal. The high winds were too terrible for the team to climb and so I was trapped at Camp 4. Climbers attempting to reach the summit of Everest spend about 8 hours resting at South Col before they head out on their final push. But because I was stuck in such a bad wind storm I was trapped at the South Col for over 52 hours, slowly dying. Wind speeds were measuring over 100 kilometres per hour. Can you imagine being in a tent, that high up, with wind speeds making it impossible to stand up? I just huddled up in my tent, wrapped in my sleeping bag and trying to save my body heat. It was about -36°C. The noise of the wind was incredible – like the roar of anger. It was absolutely pitch black. With every passing minute I thought that the tent would blow off and that my life would come to an end up there on the mountainside.'

## Ask yourself

Can you scan this text and identify **relevant** information?

## Assess your progress

- I use my finger to focus my attention.
- I move my attention from left to right.
- I keep reminding myself of what I am scanning for.
- I scan quickly but I don't rush.
- I check information I find against the question or statement.

# Making a deduction

Can you remember how to make a deduction? Can you link these words together? What is the text going to be about? Use the image and stems to help you.

→ wall → stone → drowned

→ rear → giant → crunch

→ The literal meaning of this word is …

→ This word suggests …

→ This word reminds me of …

→ This word links with …

Here are the words as they appear in the text:
- A stone wall of water rose ahead and beyond that wall reared another.
- Thunder drowned out the murmur of his prayer.
- Giant teeth of white water crunched into his mind.

## The text itself

Below are the sentences as they appear in the extract.

A stone wall of water rose ahead and beyond that wall reared another. He had never seen such a storm. Giant teeth of white water crunched into his mind. It sloshed around his bare feet. The wooden planks beneath him bulged and strained. The boat tipped and rocked under the heavy sky. He kept his eyes fixed on the ragged edges of his soaked trousers, nursing the broken hand in his lap. The angry wind tore at the roots of his grey hair while the thunder drowned out the murmur of his prayer. Such a small boat. Such a huge sea. Such a small boat. Such a vast sea.

## Getting better at making deductions

- Read the text carefully.
- Ask who/what/where/when/why/which/how questions.
- Try to answer some of those questions.
- Make links between your answers.
- Make your deduction.
- Explain it clearly.

## Ask yourself

Can you make a deduction?

Why is this man in the boat?

# Making judgements about texts

 How ...?

 What ...?

 Who ...?

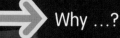 Why ...?

THE NUMBER ONE BESTSELLER

YANN MARTEL

*Life of Pi*

winner of
THE Man B

## You are learning:

How to explain which text you prefer

**How successful are you at making a deduction?**

- I read the text/image carefully.
- I ask who/what/where/when/why/which/how questions about the text/image.
- I try to answer some of those questions.
- I make links between my answers.
- I make a deduction.
- I explain my deduction clearly.

 Where ...?

 Which ...?

 When ...?

GEORGE CLOONEY

MAR
WAHLBER

FEEL
ITS
FURY

## Ask yourself

What do you think will happen in each of these stories?

 THE PERFECT STORM

Both *The Life of Pi* and *The Perfect Storm* tell the story of an adventure which takes place at sea. Based on the images, which story do you think you would prefer? Explain your choice and then give three reasons to support it.

> Another reason I would like this story is …

> To me, the story that looks like it would be most interesting is …

> One of the reasons I would like to read/watch this story is …

> Finally, I think that I would like this story best because …

**The same but different**

The two texts on the right tell **the same story**, but they tell it in different ways.

What is happening in this text? Use your deduction skills.

Now read the second text.

CRACK! The sound filled the cabin. A jolt threw her against the wheel and she found that her chest was tight. Breathe! What was happening? The deck beneath her feet was suddenly slippery. Icy coldness flooded her shoes. So cold! A different coldness gripped at her chest.

A great cracking sound filled the cabin. The sound was followed by a jolt. She was thrown against the wheel and could not breathe. She felt confused. Water already covered the deck. The water seeped into her shoes. It was so cold. She was afraid.

## Ask yourself

Which of these two texts do you find the most exciting and why?

What is the difference between these two texts?

# Making predictions

## You are learning:
How to predict and speculate

- How is the man in the picture below feeling and why?
- What might this man be thinking?

To make an inference:

1 Ask a question of the image or text.
2 Use the stems to read beneath the surface.
3 Make your inference.
4 Check your inference by looking for details to support it.

How is the man in the text below feeling and why?

- He awoke with a groan on his lips.
- It took great courage for him to open his eyes.
- He didn't understand why his knee was hurting so badly.
- Being careful not to move his leg, he drew himself up onto his elbows.
- As he looked around him, his eyes widened.
- Miles of sand met miles of ocean.
- Behind him, a forest throbbed with shadows.

## What could happen next?

As your reading skills improve, you will begin to make **predictions** about what may happen next in a story.

- Next, I think … I know this because …

- I believe … I believe this because …

- I feel that … I feel this because …

How is the man in this text feeling and why?

**Which of these images will help you to remember how to make a prediction?**

> In my mind I can see … so this makes me think …

> A frown gripped his face. He noticed that the sun was already low in the sky and that the air was cooling fast. He must find shelter. The tide had turned and soon the water would reach his feet. Bits of the ship, his old friend, lay around him. A piece of wood, which might have been part of the deck, stuck out of the sand. He had spent years polishing that deck. Dragging himself upright, he strained his eyes to see some sign of human life. Nothing. Instead, reminding himself that he was no longer a boy, he faced the forest.

> This reminds me of … because …

**WAIT!** Make a prediction before reading on.

> If this was me I would feel … because …

> The forest was dark but he reminded himself that it would be dry. Giant creepers twisted like snakes around the trunks of the trees. His heart beat like a drum in his chest. Pushing through the bushes that lined the shore, he limped into the first shadows. He turned back to look at the ink-like ocean. What if he went too far into this jungle and became lost? What if there were creatures alive and hunting amongst these trees? Beyond, where the darkness was deepest, something moved. Something. Losing his nerve, he turned on his good leg and made his way back to the shore.

> Have I checked my predictions by finding a detail in the text to back it up?

## Assess your progress

Can I ask a question of the text?
Can I read beneath the surface to answer the questions?
Can I use details from the text to back up my ideas?
Can I make a prediction?

# What will this text be about?

**You are learning:**
How to use different reading skills: infer, deduce, predict

mask
swim
power

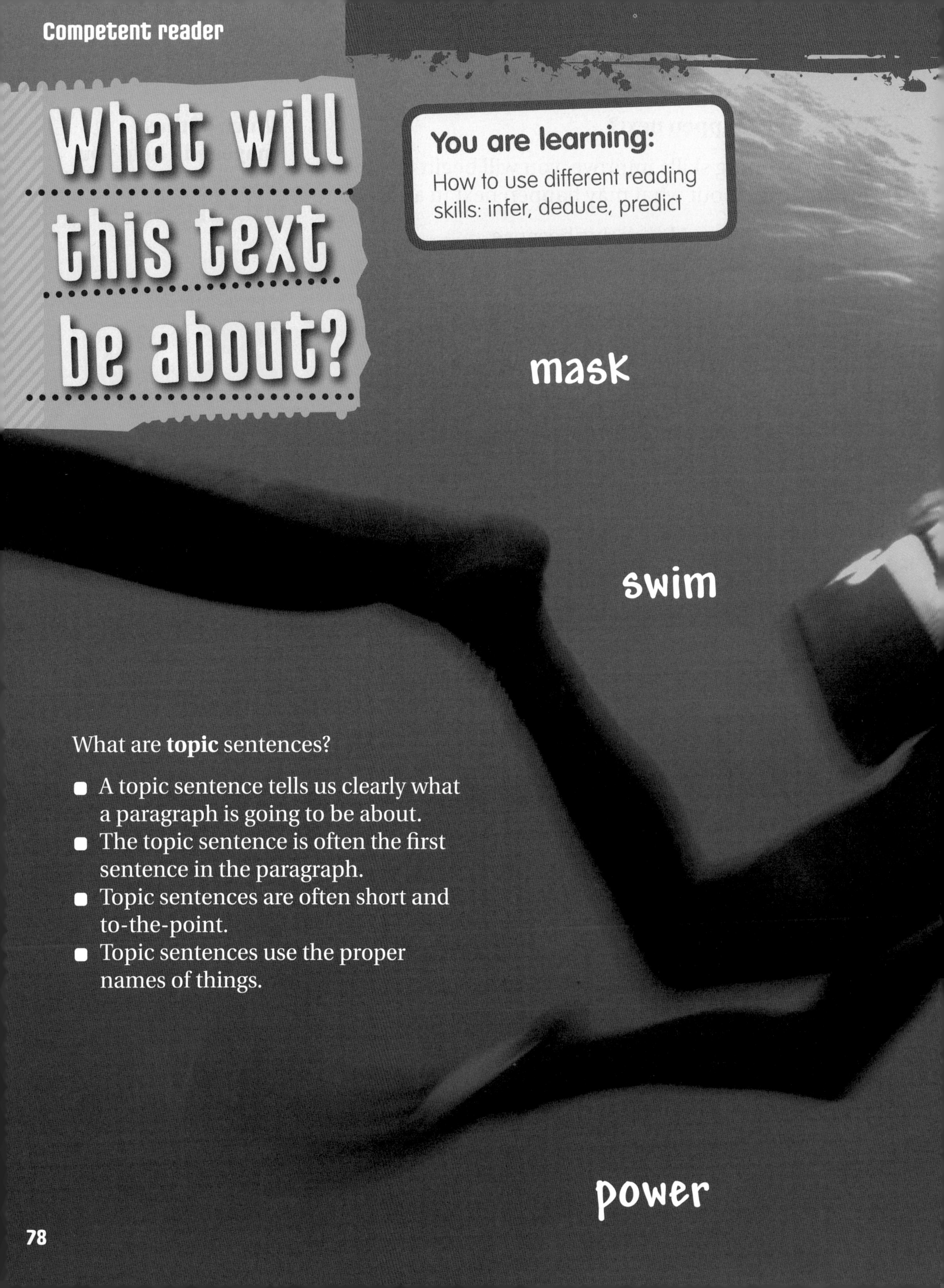

What are **topic** sentences?

- A topic sentence tells us clearly what a paragraph is going to be about.
- The topic sentence is often the first sentence in the paragraph.
- Topic sentences are often short and to-the-point.
- Topic sentences use the proper names of things.

fins

depth

pools

Which of the sentences below are topic sentences? Which of them are from the middle or ends of paragraphs?

First, the glass needs to be scratch-proof and shatter-proof.

Divers use special footwear called 'fins'.

They are essential in moving the diver through the water.

Air can be pumped into the jacket from the cylinder carried on the diver's back.

They consist of two parts: a rubber mouthpiece and rigid tube that points upward, together forming the shape of the letter 'J'.

## Ask yourself

Most texts have been written for a purpose.
- Why has this text been written?
- Who might find this text interesting?
- How might this text be useful?

# Striking a balance

...............

Adverts are texts that have two purposes. One purpose is to give us information about the thing being sold. Their main purpose, though, is to persuade us to buy the product being sold.

Where do we see adverts? Next time you see an advert, remember that adverts are a mixture of information and persuasion. Can you tell the difference?

### You are learning:

How to understand the main purpose of a text

45 exciting minutes in the water

You will love

Fun

INFORMATION

PERSUASION

Warn-signals

safety checks

## Ask yourself

Take a word/phrase from the text …
Is this word/phrase giving information or is it trying to persuade the reader?
Which side of the scales should this word/phrase go on?
How did you make your decision?

# Kids' Scuba Diving

## Ocean-flyer kids scuba for two: £45

Did you know that over 70% of the planet is covered with water? It's true, and learning to scuba dive is a fantastic way of discovering this vast and exciting underwater world.

The Ocean-flyer experience is a fun and safe way to be introduced to scuba diving in a controlled environment. All instructors are fully qualified and all equipment needed for the experience is provided. During the Ocean-flyer experience, you will master some of the basic concepts and scuba skills such as hand signals and use of equipment.

Once you get the hang of it, you will love the incredible feeling of weightlessness whilst breathing under water. It's pure magic!

## Who?

The Ocean-flyer scuba experience is open to kids aged 8 to 12 years. You must be comfortable in the water and be able to swim. You will need to have a parent/legal guardian with you to satisfactorily complete medical forms before being able to take part in the experience. Once the safety checks have been completed, the adventure begins ...

## Be prepared

You will need to bring a towel and swimwear as you will spend most of the morning in a pool. You should also bring a t-shirt to wear as you will be carrying scuba equipment. Make sure that you get a good night's sleep before the course and bring a healthy snack or two to eat between pool sessions so that you have lots of energy for your big day. Great fun can make you hungry!

## When?

Our Ocean-flyer course begins at 9 a.m. You will have a safety briefing, lasting about 30 minutes, before being kitted out. After this you will spend 45 exciting minutes in the water, followed by a break for a snack. The second out-of-this-world pool session will then begin in our cutting-edge wave pool, complete with live tropical fish, lasting a further 45 minutes. Ocean-flyer scuba sessions run throughout the year on weekdays and weekends.

# Anyone for scuba?

These photographs come from adverts for a scuba-diving holiday.

Their aim is to make people want to buy a scuba-diving holiday.

Do these pictures make **you** want to try scuba diving? If they do, then **how**?

 How do the colours used make you want to try scuba diving?

 Do the people in the picture make you want to try scuba diving? How?

Does anything else in the picture make you want to try scuba diving?

## Ask yourself

Make a choice!
- For you, which picture is most successful?
- Can you explain why?

| Give your choice | The image which makes me want to scuba dive is ... |
| --- | --- |
| Explain a reason for your choice | This image is most successful because ... |
| Use a detail from the image to back up your reason | In the image I can see ... this is important because ... |

## The ingredients of a written advert

Different text types have different shapes and ingredients. How are adverts different from other texts?

Read the advert below, advertising a scuba-diving holiday.

**2** A heading explaining what the advert is selling

**3** An opening section, grabbing the reader's attention

**4** Some text with carefully chosen words and phrases, describing what is being sold

### Get set for an adventure!

Have you ever spent an hour under the sea exploring a coral reef? Felt the freedom of life aboard a sailing yacht? Met the morning with a plunge overboard? Get ready for an incredible experience, because this is only a taste of the adventure.

**Live aboard a yacht while learning to dive and sail**

Our most popular program blends scuba and sail training with island exploration and adventure. Imagine cruising aboard a 50-foot yacht, island hopping across the Caribbean's French and Dutch West Indies with a crew of 12 teens your age. Discover the magic of scuba on coral reefs teeming with life. Throw in the Bob Marley CD, hoist the anchor and take the helm as you learn to sail on crystal blue waters. Enjoy an afternoon relaxing on a perfect white sand beach or challenge your crewmates to a friendly game of beach volleyball.

Get set for an amazing summer!

**1** An image showing the reader what the advert is selling

**5** A final attempt to win over the reader

Can you find all five of these features in this advert?

## Ask yourself

Can you place the following parts of an advert in the correct order?

### Underwater Discoveries

Most people think that becoming an Open Water Diver will cost the earth, but you will find our course surprisingly affordable. Trained by experts, you will soon be ready to experience the wonder of the underwater environment. You will learn to dive in our newly built instruction centre with a team of people your own age, building strong friendships. So, join now and enjoy being part of a community of divers.

Are you ready to begin this new chapter in your life?

Ever wished that you could fly? Well, dream can become reality when you learn to scuba dive. Soar over the sea's golden sandy bed. Float between the towering mountains of rock rising from the ocean's depths and marvel at what lies beneath the waves.

**Become an Open Water Scuba Diver and explore the underwater world.**

Which of these adverts is most likely to persuade you to buy a scuba-diving holiday?

For me _____ is the most successful advert.

My first reason is ...

Secondly ...

Finally, I think ...

## Assess your progress

Do I know how an advert might begin?
Do I know where a heading might be used?
Do I know how an advert might end?
Can I explain how the advert persuades me?

85

# Active reader!

## You are learning:
To use your reading strategies independently

- When you read this text, what do you 'see' or imagine?
- Which words and phrases create the strongest mind pictures for you?

- When you read this text, which bits do you most like? Which ideas do you most easily understand?
- Is there anything in the text that you dislike or ideas that you don't understand?
- Can you understand what the characters in the text are doing and thinking? Would you want to be in their shoes?

- What do you already know about this topic that might help you understand the text?
- Have you come across a story like this before?
- What do you think might happen in this story and what are the clues that tell you?

- When you read this text, what more do you want to find out?
- Is there anything that puzzles or interests you?
- What 5W questions would it be useful to ask to find out more about events and characters? (Who, What, Where, When, Why)

Why...? This makes me feel... Perhaps... What...?

I can imagine what it must be like to... How...? At this point in the text, in my mind I can see... Will the character...?

This makes me wonder... If this was happening to me... The word _____ helps me to imagine the place where this text is set... Maybe...? Who...? Is it possible that...?

**Test yourself!**

Use your active reading strategies to work out
what is happening in this text. Try out the strategies
one at a time, reading through the text each time.
After using each strategy, talk with a partner about
the meaning you have found.

As I had planned, I was the first to reach the entrance of the cave. It looked
to me like a huge mouth yawning, as though something deep in the rock
was waking up. I was breathing heavily and slumped down against the
rock-face. All around me was a sea of thick tree-tops and beyond that the
blue of the ocean itself. The climb had been steep and I needed to rest,
but I was also excited and could not prevent myself from standing up and
glancing back down the hillside. Was he behind me? Each time I looked,
the pathway I had cut between the twisted trunks was empty. I soon grew
certain that he was lost in the undergrowth or lying exhausted somewhere.
You see, he was so much older than me and had spent years studying in
the libraries of the university. The day's trek would have caused him great
difficulty, if he had made it at all. I smiled. If he didn't find the cave, I would
not have to explain my actions to him.

## Ask yourself

How did your reading go?
- Which of the reading strategies helped you to find the **most** meaning?
- Which of the reading strategies helped you to find the most **interesting**
  meanings?
- Which of these strategies would you use **first** when reading a new text? Why?
- Which of these strategies would you leave until **last** when reading a new text?
  Why?

# Betrayal

**You are learning:**
How to independently use your reading strategies

Remind yourself:

- What has already happened in this story?
- What questions did you have about the story as you read?
- How did the story make you feel?
- What pictures did you have in your mind as you read?
- What predictions did you make about what would happen next?

## Ask yourself

How is the narrator feeling? Why?

My mind was spinning. As the minutes passed, I tried to calm myself for long enough to make the decision. I turned the situation over and over in my mind, looking at it one way and then another. This morning, as our ship had pulled towards the shore, I had already stolen the map of the island from his bag. But I could have explained this by saying that I was excited about the trip ahead and wanted to look at the map once again. The old man trusted me so well; I had seen this trust every day for years in his veined blue eyes. I knew that he would even forgive me for running away from him into the jungle as soon as our feet had touched the sandy shore. But to enter this cave without him, to begin the search alone, was different. For this I would never be forgiven.

But would I need him any more? For years he had found me jobs which had provided me with a little money each month. It was he who had found me the tiny room in the university grounds where I slept each night. But every night for years I had dreamed of having more. If the information on the map I held in my hand was correct, I would never need anybody ever again. With this thought, my chest rose and my back straightened. Gold and silver pieces rained down in my mind.

I was standing on the knife-edge of the biggest decision I had ever made. If I chose to go alone into the cave, my life would be changed forever. Already the sun was lower in the sky and time was running out. If the map was correct, and my careful calculations were right, I would take two hours to reach the inner chamber and return with my prize. By then it would already be night and I would have to camp on the hillside until dawn. As soon as it grew light I would have to hurry back to the shore to meet the boat. The timing would be very tight – a single mistake and I might not make it back in time to the shore. What if I had made an error in my calculations? What if the map itself was incorrect? These questions multiplied with great speed and chewed into my calm like jagged teeth.

## Assess your progress

Can I make a successful response to this text?

- Can I make a clear point about the text which answers the question I have been asked?
- Can I explain *why* I think what I do?
- Can I *find* a word or phrase in the text to back up my idea?
- Can I *use* this word or phrase to back up my idea?

# A struggle of the mind

Remember:

What has happened in this story so far?

> The old man trusted me so well.

> But every night for years I had dreamed of having more.

> I would never need anybody ever again.

Be true to the old man

> For years he had found me jobs which had provided me with a little money each month.

> For this I would never be forgiven.

## Ask yourself

Should the narrator enter the cave without the old man?

**90**

Gold and silver pieces rained down in my mind.

Betray the old man

I had seen this trust every day for years.

# Ask yourself

How can I make a personal response to the text?

- I make sure that I understand the question.
- I can think carefully about the different responses that I could make.
- I can choose the response that I prefer.
- I can find evidence from the text to help me explain my preference/personal response.
- I can explain the reasons behind my ideas.

What could happen next?

What do you remember about how to make a prediction?

- Re-read the text carefully.

- Find clues placed in the text by the writer: what might happen next?

- Come up with some ideas. Think them through carefully.

- Make sure that you can find some evidence in the text to show where your prediction comes from.

- Make your prediction and explain it clearly.

As I stood at the mouth of the cave that evening, I did not notice that the ground was cleared of plants and trees. I was too overcome with excitement about what lay within this giant rock to notice the charred remains of firewood a little way to the left. It would not be until I was standing outside the cave once more, some three terrifying hours later, that I would recognise these things as signs warning DISASTER. At the time, I could think only of a future draped in gold. So, with my head torch beam on half-power and the map unfolded in my hands, I took one last look at the angry-red horizon and plunged into the cave's darkness.

# Making notes

Blue face – different from the others. So, is he the hero?

Can't see this man's face – not the hero.

## You are learning:

How to make notes on a text

As your reading improves, you will find that you have ideas about the meaning of a text **as** you are reading. One way to make sure that you remember these ideas is to make notes about the text **as** you read. We call this 'annotation'.

Make a **deduction**: Who is the hero in this image and how can you tell?

A student who was asked this question made notes around the picture as they were thinking. Which note relates to which part of the image?

Lots of men.

Long hair.

These men are further back. The hero would be at the front of the picture.

Why is he doing this?

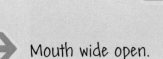 This man is leaning forward, ready for battle. But can't see much of his body.

→ Mouth wide open.

→ Strong hands.

→ A battle is about to begin?

→ This man is leaning back. I think the hero would be leaning forward.

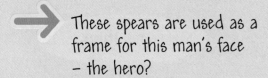 These spears are used as a frame for this man's face – the hero?

## Ask yourself

**Practise your note-making skills**

Deduce: What has just happened to this character?

Infer: How does he feel?

Predict: What is he about to do?

## Assess your progress

Am I a successful note-maker?
- I only make notes that will answer the question.
- I keep my notes short so that they don't take too long to write.
- I make sure that my notes are clear so that I can understand them later.
- I record my thinking so that I will remember my thoughts later on.

# The writer's choices

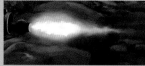

slicing of bullets

twisted lives

clash of metal

cruel wire

## You are learning:

How to comment on the words a writer uses

In the same way as artists carefully select the colours of the paint that they use, writers think carefully about the words that they choose.

Writers choose words that will:

- affect the way their readers **feel**.
- shape the way their readers **think**.
- help their readers to **understand** the main ideas of the text.

The phrases here are taken from the first verse of a poem called 'The Hero'. They have been carefully chosen by the writer. What do you think they are describing? What do you think they might mean?

Can you make any links or connections between these phrases?

What do you think this poem is going to be about?

You could say:

- 'Perhaps …'
- 'I wonder if …'
- 'It is possible that …'

What do these words 'do' to the reader?

Makes me **question** …

**The hero**
Who is it that calls me a hero?
How would they know? Were they there?
Did they hear the clash of metal on metal?
Did they feel the slicing of bullets through air?
Did they see the twisted lives of men hanging
    on cruel wire,
Of men who were boys just yesterday?

Makes me **feel** …

Helps me to **understand** …

Leads me to **wonder** if …

Makes me **think** …

## Which words would you choose?

Here is the second verse of the poem, 'The Hero'. Three of the most powerful words have been replaced with blanks.

Read through the verse and try to come up with three suggestions for each blank, before choosing the most powerful one.

Who is it that calls me a hero?
How would they know? Were they there?
Did they hear the order to march into _____?
Did they have to swallow their _____ fear,
Standing with the tips of their toes overhanging
That _____ of terror?

## Ask yourself

Can you explain why you chose the words you did?
- How will your chosen words make the reader feel?
- What will they help the reader to understand?
- How will these words shape your reader's thoughts?

# How can we tell?

## You are learning:

How to use quotations to support your ideas

### The hero

Who is it that calls me a hero?
How would they know? Were they there?
Did they hear the clash of metal on metal?
Did they feel the slicing of bullets through air?
Did they see the twisted lives of men hanging on
   cruel wire,
Of men who were boys just yesterday?

Who is it that calls me a hero?
How would they know? Were they there?
Did they hear the order to march into darkness?
Did they have to swallow their gaping fear,
Standing with the tips of their toes overhanging
That cliff of terror?

## Ask yourself

- How can we tell that war was dangerous?
- How can we tell that many men died?
- How can we tell that the soldiers were frightened?
- How does the poet show that war is a waste of life?

## How to use a quotation

**1** Read the question carefully.

**2** Think about the kind of evidence that you will be looking for.

**3** Scan the text for evidence to answer the question.

**4** Select a word/phrase as evidence.

**5** Use the wording of the question to help you answer it.

**5** Place your evidence inside quotation marks.

### How does this soldier feel?

Is it you that calls me a hero?
How would you know? Were you there?
You didn't see me hide my face from the
    boom of shells,
You didn't feel the drum of panic in my heart
As men reached out for help.
How can I be called 'hero'?
I returned home, they still lie there.

You can't call me a hero
Because I've been decorated with medals.
Discs of dull metal don't make me a hero;
The real heroes are still lying there.

## Assess your progress

- Can I say which words have been carefully chosen by the writer?
- Can I say what these words make me 'see' in my mind?
- Can I say what these words make me 'hear' in my mind?
- Can I make links between these words and things that have happened to me?
- Can I ask questions about these words?

# Recording your findings

Here are two different texts about the same event: a young tennis player winning an international competition. You have heard on the radio that a match was won, but you want more details. To find out more, you are going to carry out some research.

You want to know:

- **Who** won the match.

- **Where** the match was being played.

- **What** happened during the match.

- **When** the victory happened.

As you read, how will you record the useful information that you find?

# Macnally's heroic victory

**Ryan Macnally proved that he could be Britain's next champion by winning his first Wimbledon match in straight sets this afternoon.**

In spite of suffering an injury to his ankle in the first ten minutes of the game, 18-year-old Macnally played with skill and determination. Playing in front of a crowd of 5000 excited spectators, he won the first set comfortably. But Macnally's opponent, experienced Spanish player Juan Rodrigues, who came second in the Australian Open last year, fought back and won the first four games of the second set in a row. However, Macnally's spirit was superb and he soon re-found his confidence.

The third and fourth sets were wonderful to watch. Macnally's powerful serve and his lightning speed set the crowd on Number 1 court roaring and waving Union Jack flags between every point played. By 4.32 p.m. Macnally's superb victory was complete and he left the court triumphant.

After the match, the young Londoner, who has been playing tennis since he was just three years old, admitted that he was surprised with his win.

'I went into the match hoping to win at least one set but I didn't imagine that I would beat Rodrigues. He is such a good player. After the first set I felt great. But I must admit that my nerves got the better of me for a while after that. I am delighted with the win.'

When asked to comment on his fitness, he played down his injury.

'My ankle was painful at the time but I just had to block it out of my mind. After half an hour, the pain was gone and I could play at my best. After the first set, winning was the only thing on my mind.'

Macnally is now through to round 3 of the competition and plays again in two days. His coach, Len Mason, says, 'Ryan has a strict timetable of practice for the next two days. He will be on the practice courts for three hours each morning. After that, he will spend some relaxing time with his family.'

Sporting experts are already describing Ryan as the most promising young player on the courts this year.

# What a fantastic day: one to remember.

My nerves were ragged even before Ryan emerged from the dressing rooms. It still seems very strange watching my little brother walking onto one of the most famous tennis courts in the world. I don't know how he keeps so calm, with the journalists' cameras pointing at his every move and the TV cameras lined up along the edge. But he does keep so calm. It's amazing!

The match began at 12.15 p.m., bang on time. I wanted to call out and wish Ryan luck like I used to do when he was playing for the local club as a kid. But times have changed and things are a lot more serious now, so I kept quiet and crossed fingers, arms, legs and toes for luck instead. Mum and Dad were in the seats next to mine, in the front row of seats above the dressing rooms. As the umpire called for quiet, I looked along the row. Mum's mouth was drawn into a straight line and Dad was leaning forward in his seat as though he was about to run a race. Even though they have been to every single one of Ryan's matches since he began competing, they both looked ill.

When Ryan hurt his ankle - and he really did fall on it heavily, crying out as he landed - I thought that it was game-over. It was his weaker ankle: the one he injured last summer. Amazingly though, he picked himself up and kept on playing. He limped a bit but within minutes was back on form. There was one other scare in the match: the beginning of the second set when he seemed to lose his concentration. Ryan has been playing so well but none of us expected him to beat Rodrigues. One by one, Ryan lost a series of games. His confidence started to fail him. I remember looking at the clock: 1.03 p.m. This is it, I thought. The muscles in his neck became really tight, so I knew that he was stressed. Mum kept whispering, 'Keep calm, Ryan, keep calm.' I could barely breathe. It was so hot. The thermometer read 27 degrees and there was no wind to stir up the air at all. It was too hot to sit still, never mind leap around the Number 1 court at Wimbledon, playing against one of the world's best players!

But he turned it round with that serve of his; some of his serves were registering 131 mph. They flew like bullets! My little brother, the champion! I shouldn't have doubted him.

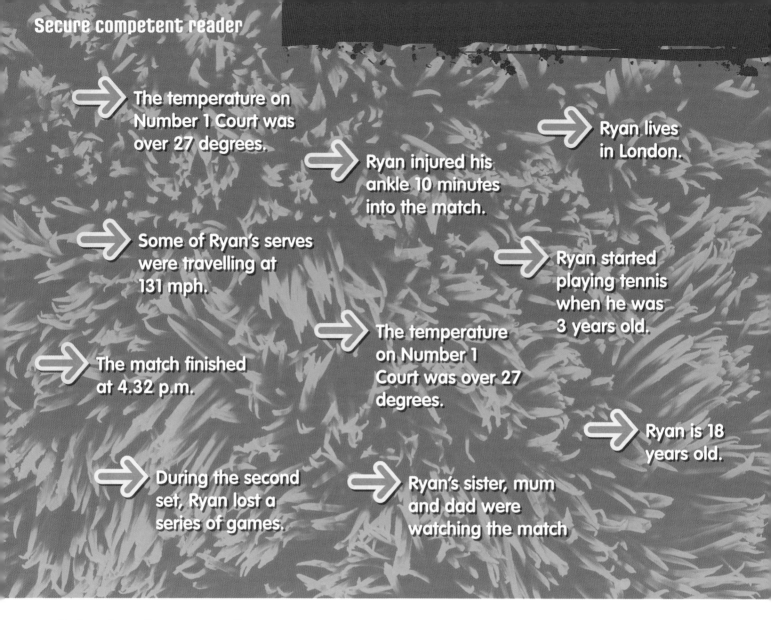

The temperature on Number 1 Court was over 27 degrees.

Ryan injured his ankle 10 minutes into the match.

Ryan lives in London.

Some of Ryan's serves were travelling at 131 mph.

Ryan started playing tennis when he was 3 years old.

The match finished at 4.32 p.m.

The temperature on Number 1 Court was over 27 degrees.

Ryan is 18 years old.

During the second set, Ryan lost a series of games.

Ryan's sister, mum and dad were watching the match

## Selecting the correct fact

When looking for information in a text to back up an idea, it is important to be able to select a fact that **fits** the question you are answering.

- Read the question and <u>underline</u> the key words.
- Think ahead: What type of fact am I looking for? What will it 'look like' on the page?
- Scan the text for relevant facts.
- Choose the most fitting fact.
- Check back with the question: Does this fact answer the question?

Now answer the questions below.

**1** At which point in the match did Ryan injure himself?

**2** How long has Ryan been playing tennis?

**3** Which set in the match was the most difficult for Ryan?

Now return to the two texts to scan for evidence to answer the following questions. Make sure that you follow the process you have been shown.

**A** How many people were watching the match on Number 1 Court?

**B** Is Rodrigues a good player?

**C** At what time did Ryan's confidence start to fail him?

**D** Was this match the first time that Ryan had hurt his ankle?

**Interview Ryan!**

When we read, it is important to be able to decide whether statements about a text are true or false.

If we think that a statement is true, we need to find facts in the text to back it up. If we think it is false, we need to find facts in the text to prove this.

Ryan will be interviewed at a press conference after his match. Read the questions that the reporters plan to ask, and say whether the statements in them are **true** or **false**.

- Ryan, is it true to say that you won this match easily?

- We understand that your ankle injury gave you a great deal of pain for the entire match, Ryan. Is that right?

- Is it true, Ryan, that you will be practising with your coach solidly between now and your next match?

- Ryan, we have heard that your family are a big support to you in your tennis career. Is this right?

## Ask yourself

What will Ryan answer?

No, actually that is not quite right ... In fact I ...

Yes, you are correct ... I ...

Find facts from the text to support your answers.

# what do we mean by 'the structure of a text'?

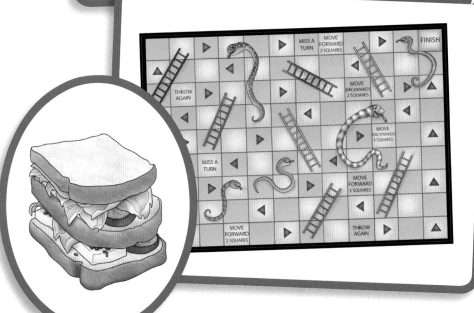

Above the main room lies a sleeping nest

This cage has three different 'rooms'

This box connects with the main cage via a plastic tube

## You are learning:

How to identify the main features of a text

When we talk about the structure of something, we mean:

- how it is shaped
- how it is laid out
- how it is ordered
- how it is organised
- how its parts are linked or held together
- how one part of it is important to another part
- how it has been put together.

**Investigation:**
Describe what you notice about the way these things are structured. The description of the first image might give you some ideas.

You could say:

First …      Secondly …
To the right …   To the left … Above …    Below …

This links with …
This connects to …
The most important part is … because …

# Macnally's heroic victory

**Ryan Macnally proved that he could be Britain's next champion by winning his first Wimbledon match in straight sets this afternoon.**

In spite of suffering an injury to his ankle in the first ten minutes of the game, 18-year-old Macnally played with skill and determination. Playing in front of a crowd of 5000 excited spectators, he won the first set comfortably. But Macnally's opponent, experienced Spanish player Juan Rodrigues, who came second in the Australian Open last year, fought back and won the first four games of the second set in a row. However, Macnally's spirit was superb and he soon re-found his confidence.

### Lightning speed

The third and fourth sets were wonderful to watch. Macnally's powerful serve and his lightning speed set the crowd on Number 1 court roaring and waving Union Jack flags between every point played. By 4.32 p.m. Macnally's superb victory was complete and he left the court triumphant.

After the match, the young Londoner, who has been playing tennis since he was just three years old, admitted that he was surprised with his win.

'I went into the match hoping to win at least one set but I didn't imagine that I would beat Rodrigues. He is such a good player. After the first set I felt great. But I must admit that my nerves got the better of me for a while after that. I am delighted with the win.'

When asked to comment on his fitness, he played down his injury.

'My ankle was painful at the time but I just had to block it out of my mind. After half an hour, the pain was gone and I could play at my best. After the first set, winning was the only thing on my mind.'

### Strict discipline

Macnally is now through to round 3 of the competition and plays again in two days. His coach, Len Mason, says, 'Ryan has a strict timetable of practice for the next two days. Discipline is very important for young players. He will be on the practice courts for 3 hours each morning. After that, he will spend some relaxing time with his family.'

Sporting experts are already describing Ryan as the most promising young player on the courts this year.

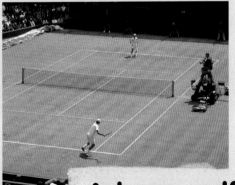

## Ask yourself

Can you match these descriptions with parts of the newspaper report?

- Headline: 7 words or less. In capital letters.

- Topic sentence: 21 words or less. Tells reader WHO is involved, WHERE events took place, WHAT happened and WHEN it happened.

- Main report: more detail about HOW and WHY the events happened.

- Cross heading: to introduce the next part of the report and to make it exciting.

- Reported speech: what people said when questioned about events.

- Final sentence: rounding up the report. Summary of situation.

- Photograph of an aspect of the incident.

# Dramatic language

## You are learning:
How to understand a writer's choice of words

As you already know, a newspaper report is centred around key facts about an event. These facts tell us who, where, what and when. The following facts are taken from a newspaper report about a fire at a family home:

**Who:** a family of five: mother, father, three children

**Where:** at the family home, down a track outside a village

**What:** a fire

**When:** late on Saturday night

**How:** a damaged electric cable

Writers choose their words carefully: newspapers make a lot of money and exciting stories sell newspapers.

If you were a writer, which words would you use to make the events seem more dramatic and exciting?

For example:

| Who FACT | → | three children |
|---|---|---|

| Which word? | → | young tiny vulnerable frightened |
|---|---|---|

# RAGING FIRE ENDANGERS FAMILY

**A young family narrowly escaped from a fire at their home last night.**

The Taylors, Samuel (32), his wife Karen (27) and their three tiny children were all fast asleep upstairs in their isolated cottage when the fast-spreading fire broke out on the landing. Karen, who has just given birth to the family's third child, woke choking to a room filled with deadly smoke at around midnight. She screamed to her husband to

Which of these words would you choose if you wanted to make the event seem dramatic and terrible?

WHO:
young
tiny
vulnerable
frightened

WHAT:
devastating
deadly
terrible
fast-spreading
lightning-quick

WHEN:
late
dark

HOW:
lethal
murderous
dangerous

WHERE:
deserted
far-removed
isolated
little-known
out-of-reach

## Ask yourself

Can you explain how a word might make a fact more exciting or dramatic?

- Can you explain how the word makes you feel?
- Can you explain what the word reminds you of?
- Can you explain what the word makes you 'see' or 'hear'?
- Can you draw your ideas together and say why the writer has used that word?

save the two older children who were stranded in the other bedroom. Samuel discovered that the fire had already taken a stranglehold of the landing. The quick-thinking couple stripped the bed, poured a jug of water over a sheet and wrapped it around Samuel's upper body and face. He then plunged into the flames towards his little ones' bedroom.

Meanwhile Karen lowered herself out of the main bedroom's window onto the roof of the porch, with her newborn tied with pillow cases to her chest.

### Quick-thinking

Karen, a nursery nurse, was surprised at how clearly she was thinking during this nightmare.

'Samuel was so calm and brave. I knew that I could trust him to get across the landing and into the bedroom. I knew that I had to get the baby away from the smoke. We have talked before about what we would do if there was a fire at the cottage. We had a plan and we followed it.'

The emergency services were called shortly after midnight by a neighbour who had seen the flames in the darkness. Even though the Taylors' cottage is 5 miles outside the nearest town and situated down a rough farm track, the fire engine was there within 10 minutes, in time to lower Samuel and the two toddlers from the second bedroom window. Both children suffered smoke inhalation with minor burns to the hands. Samuel's injuries were more serious, although he is expected to be out of hospital by the end of the week.

The fire, thought to have been caused by a damaged electric cable, destroyed the top half of the house before firefighters could get the blaze under control.

### Lethal

Police investigators described the damaged cable running from an electric fire on the landing of the house as lethal. Police Constable Jenny Wright said, 'We must take more responsibility to repair damage to electrical equipment. The Taylors are lucky to have escaped with minor injuries.' It is thought that the family's dog had chewed through the cable the previous weekend and it hadn't yet been repaired.

# Getting better at research

## You are learning:
How to find and record information

Kate has just started Year 10; she is interested in being a firefighter. She has had her first interview with the school's Careers Advisor, who wants Kate to do some research about the job.

When we research we must read with a purpose. We need to know:

- **Why** we are reading.
- **What** we are looking for.
- **How** we are going to read.
- **How** we are going to record the information that we find.

## A DAY IN THE LIFE OF A FIREFIGHTER

A firefighter's day might start in the middle of the night. Firefighters have to respond at top speed at any time of the day or night, in any weather conditions, acting sensibly and calmly and with safety always in mind.

Firefighters might find themselves at the site of a road accident, rescuing someone from a smoke-filled building, talking to primary school children about what to do in case of a fire or giving first aid and comfort to the victim of a flood.

But the firefighter has to be prepared for anything. Although lots of training is provided, firefighters often find themselves in situations that no-one can prepare them for. At these times, teamwork and problem-solving skills are very important.

## Ask yourself

**What** does Kate want to know about firefighting?
**What** should Kate look for as she researches?
**How** should Kate read as she researches?
**How** should Kate record the information she finds?

Kate finds this in a leaflet about becoming a firefighter:

Kate finds this on a website about becoming a firefighter:

**HOME**

**NEWS**

**PHOTO GALLERY**

**CONTACT US**

## Can you make your community a safer place?

Do you see yourself sliding down a pole and jumping into a gleaming red fire engine? Then screaming off into the night, lights flashing and sirens blazing? If you think that this is what a firefighter does for a living, then forget it!

Being a firefighter is not just about responding to fires and other emergencies, it's so much more. Firefighters have to work to prevent fires from starting. They do this by taking safety messages into schools, businesses and communities. By teaching people about being safe, firefighters can stop fires happening in the first place and save lives.

To succeed as a firefighter you should be a team player who is friendly and can work well with others. You should be able to remain calm when under pressure. You need to be confident in a variety of situations.

## Assess your progress

- Before reading, do I make sure that I know why I am reading?

- Can I scan for specific information?

- Can I make useful notes on the information I find?

- Can I use the notes I have made?

# Point of view

## You are learning:

How to recognise a writer's point of view

- What does 'point of view' mean?

- What does it mean when we talk about a writer's 'point of view'?

Lord Nelson was a famous British war hero. Just over two hundred years ago he led a series of important battles defending Britain in a war against France. In one of these battles he was badly injured and died. Even though he died, Britain still won the battle. Nelson has been considered a hero ever since, and many artists have painted pictures of his death.

The painters of these pictures of Nelson share a point of view: they both had positive views about Nelson.

**Point of view:** Nelson was a good man

**A** Nelson was a great leader, loved by his men

**B** Nelson was a brave man

**C** Nelson was a very important man in British history

Look closely at the images on the opposite page. What evidence is there to support each of the points of view? Look at:

- objects in the pictures.
- people in the pictures: their bodies and their faces.
- the colours used by the artist.

You could use these phrases to help you explain your findings:

This artist's view of Nelson is …

I can tell that this artist believes that Nelson is _____ because …

A detail in the picture which supports this view point is …

The following sentences are taken from a story told from the point of view of one of Nelson's men. This sailor was on Nelson's flagship when news that Nelson had been fatally wounded spread about the ship.

**1** As he lay there, precious blood draining from his body onto the wooden boards of the ship, the hope in my heart died.

**2** Although his life was seeping away and he must have been in great pain, he did not fall to the deck.

**3** Nelson, my lord, was greeted by angels and welcomed into heaven.

**4** I felt lost.

## Ask yourself

What is this writer's view of Nelson? Can you back up your answer with a word from the sentences?

## Assess your progress

Can I show that I understand a writer's viewpoint?

|  | Yes, I can | I'm nearly there | Not yet |
|---|---|---|---|
| I can understand the writer's viewpoint |  |  |  |
| I can find and pull out details in the text which show the viewpoint of the writer |  |  |  |
| I can clearly explain the writer's viewpoint, giving evidence from the text to support my explanation |  |  |  |

Which of these images could stand for a writer's point of view? Which of these images might help you to remember what we mean when we talk about a writer's 'viewpoint'?

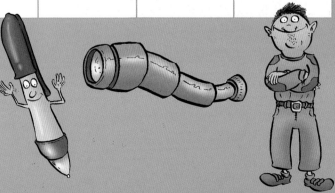

# Support your understanding of a writer's viewpoint

## You are learning:

How to back up your comments about a text

You can do this in different ways. You might make a direct quotation by taking a key word or phrase from the text. But when you want to use a larger chunk of the text as evidence, you can **paraphrase**. This means summarising or retelling a relevant part of the text to support a point or an idea.

To help you to paraphrase, use: *'I can tell this when …'* or *'I feel like this because …'*

As he lay there, precious blood draining from his body onto the wooden boards of the ship, the hope in my heart died. How could we fight this battle without our leader? How could I continue to believe that we would win?

From where I was standing absolutely still with the rest of the crew, I could see that his face was as grey as a snow-filled sky. But, even though his life was seeping away and he must have been in great pain, he did not fall to the deck. Instead he continued to give battle orders, his voice still holding strong. Supported by his officers, Admiral Lord Nelson, my lord, was greeted by angels and welcomed into heaven.

I was lost. England was lost. I fell to my knees and, under the dark sky, I raised my hands to my face and prayed that England would not be lost to the enemy. The words of my prayer tumbled out of my mouth while tears fell from my eyes.

How does the narrator feel about Nelson dying?

I think that the narrator feels frightened when Nelson dies. **I can tell this when** he kneels and prays for England's safety.

How can we tell that Nelson's injuries are serious?
How does the writer make Nelson seem like a hero?
What makes this story sad?
After reading this text, how do **you** feel about Nelson?

## Ask yourself

Can you follow all the steps below to paraphrase a text?

**1** I read the question carefully and make sure that I understand it.

**2** I scan the text for information that will help me to answer the question.

**3** I make notes for later use.

**4** I look back at the notes I have made and decide on my answer.

**5** I decide which chunk of the story helps to support my answer.

**6** I paraphrase the part of the story I have identified and use it to support my understanding.

This is also the story of Nelson's death, but the writer of this story has a very different viewpoint.

I watched him die, and with him died his cruelty and his madness. For years he had barked orders, calling for men to sacrifice their lives for him. For years he had ordered punishments to the men on his ships. I had seen boys whipped and beaten for crimes no more serious than stealing extra food to fill their hungry bellies. I remembered the lash of the whip on my own skin.

All around me I could hear the shock of the crew; Admiral Lord Nelson was injured. We stopped hoisting the ship's sails, we stopped loading the guns. We watched. In fact, it was clear that his injuries were serious. This monster, who had controlled us with fear for so many years, was slumped helpless and pale.

We watched as his blood seeped away. He still managed to issue orders in that thin, hard voice of his. His words still bullied us onwards, to fight the enemy. Then Admiral Lord Nelson breathed his final breath.

My mouth remained shut and I kept my eyes blank, but in my heart I cheered.

- How does the narrator of this story feel about Nelson?

- According to the narrator, how did Nelson treat his men?

- How do the rest of the crew act when they learn of Nelson's injuries.

- After reading this text, how do you feel about Nelson?

# Communicating a viewpoint

**silence**

**golden**

**muscle**

**sunk**

**never**

### You are learning:

How to make comments about a writer's point of view

**pain**

**raise**

Writers choose their words carefully in order to put across their viewpoint to the reader. As good readers, we need to consider what a writer's viewpoint is and how it has been communicated to us.

**1** Which of the words and images on this page would you use if you wanted to put across the viewpoint that war is heroic? Choose five words or images and explain the thinking behind each decision.

**2** Which of these words and images would you use if you wanted to put across the viewpoint that war is a waste of life? Choose five words or images and explain the thinking behind each decision.

**high**

**lower**

**order**

He knew that he would die. The pain in his chest pressed upon him, squeezing his breath into shallow gasps. His mind raced over the possible battle options, still calculating a victory. He was aware of his men waiting around him in silence for his order. He could feel their complete trust in him: he was their expert. Their eyes were trained upon him – on the seams of his jacket, the golden buckle of his boot, the slope of his forehead. The sailors drank him in.

Vast dark clouds had gathered overhead, frowning down upon the bloody battle. Pulling the jacket of his uniform straight, he raised his face to the flag soaring high above the deck. The muscles in his shoulders were still strong, his hair was not yet grey, his skin was still young. His mind held a thousand pieces of expert knowledge which would never now be shared. This man understood the waves and knew the power of the wind like no other man. This knowledge would be lost with him, like treasure sunk in the ocean.

His officers encircled him. Their hearts were already heavy with loss, but he no longer noticed them. In his mind he wrote a letter to his wife and children that would never be delivered. He was no longer aware of the clouds of gunpowder smoke blocking out the light. As he died, the sailors did not hear the boom of the guns from the enemy ships.

## The writer's viewpoint

- The writer believes that Nelson died a hero.
  TRUE or FALSE?
- The writer believes that Nelson's death was a terrible waste of life.
  TRUE or FALSE?

The sailors don't care for their captain

The sailors love their captain

Read the quotations below. For each one, say what the key word is and where it should go on the line.

*their hearts were already heavy with loss*

*he could feel their complete trust in him*

*he was aware of his men waiting in silence for his order*

*his officers encircled him*

*the sailors drank him in*

*their eyes were trained upon him*

## Assess your progress

Can I comment on the writer's use of language?
- Can I identify a word that the writer has carefully chosen?
- Can I explain why the word is important?
- Can I explain what this word helped me to understand?
- Can I say why the writer has used this word?

What target should I set myself for commenting on a writer's use of language?

# Can you choose a relevant quotation?

Look at the quotations on this page and say which ones are relevant to each of the points about Superman.

- Superman is incredibly strong

  'He flew at lightning speed.'

  'The metal bent between his fingers.'

  'His eyes were dark pools.'

  'He flexed the muscles in his chest.'

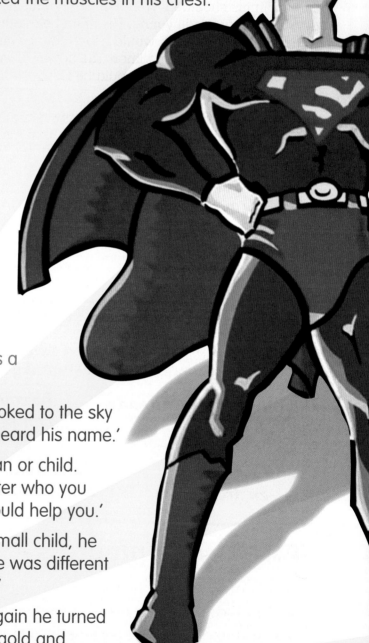

**You are learning:**

How to choose quotations to support your comments

**1** Read the statement or question carefully and underline the key words.

▼

**2** Scan the text for relevant quotations to support the question or statement.

▼

**3** Select a quotation.

▼

**4** Check back with the statement – does the quotation fit the statement well? [YES, on to 5, NO back to 2]

▼

**5** Pull the quotation from the text and present it.

- Superman is a good man

  'Everyone looked to the sky when they heard his name.'

  'Man, woman or child. It didn't matter who you were, he would help you.'

  'Even as a small child, he knew that he was different from others.'

  'Time and again he turned his back on gold and riches in order to save a life.'

- Superman was well known in his home town

'There was a picture of him on the front of every newspaper.'

'The child had cried for help and Superman had responded.'

'Every time an accident occurred, people looked to the sky and waited for his arrival.'

'His name was like bread and butter.'

Worried about the world going to waste? Terrified that the air is getting too polluted to breathe? Fear not, because Enviro-man is at hand.

If you're buried under plastic and tin cans, call Enviro-man. With arms as strong as the steel cans he recycles, Enviro-man will help you to collect your glass and take it to the bottlebank. His hearing is so sharp that he can hear an environmental disaster from 100 miles away. No oil spill is too large, no forest fire too powerful for Enviro-man.

eNVIRO-man

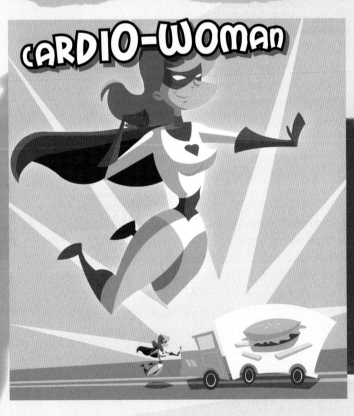

CARDIO-WOMAN

Britain's answer to the problem of heart disease. She hijacks lorries full of fast-food products on their way to football grounds and sends lettuce and cabbage instead. She bursts into people's houses and orders them out of their armchairs to exercise instead.

Even through the thickest coat or jumper, with her x-ray vision Cardio-woman can spot a human heart in need of care. No more huffing and puffing as you walk up the stairs: Cardio-woman can whip a body into good shape in the fastest time.

**1** Which of these heroes is the more daring?

**2** Which of these heroes would you most like to meet?

**3** Which of these heroes would be the most useful to the world?

Can you support your answers with a relevant question from the texts?

# Spiderman madness

Before I met Karl Metlock, I knew a few facts about Spiderman: he can stick to walls and he swings around on the end of a spider's thread. It wasn't until I entered Karl's basement bedroom at his parents' home in Leeds that I realised just how much more there is to know and love about this sticky superhero.

We all have interests. Some people are into sport. Some people follow the fortunes of their favourite band, travelling miles to see them play live. But few people have an interest as strong as 14-year-old Karl Metlock, possibly Spiderman's greatest fan.

Karl had been lonely at school and seemed bored at home so his uncle lent him a set of Spiderman comics in October 2003. 'I was 10 years old and I'd only pick up a book if I was forced to. In fact, I wasn't really interested in anything at all. Suddenly, though, I couldn't stop reading. All I could think about was getting hold of the next Spiderman comic. I was hooked.' Every Saturday morning, Karl would get out of bed without being called. By 9 a.m. he could be found searching through second-hand shops, looking for more comics. It was around this time that he discovered his first Spiderman outfit and a series of plastic Spiderman figures. Karl cleared a shelf in his room to display the items he bought. The collection had begun!

But Karl didn't stop at collecting Spiderman objects or watching the films. Before long, he had rigged up a rope system in the back garden of his home to practise his rope-swings. He even began to develop a super-strength glue which he hoped to apply to his hands and feet and stick himself to walls like his hero.

'At first, I was a bit concerned,' Sharon Metlock explains. He would disappear for hours at a time in the workshop at the back of the house. We tried to put a padlock on the door but he was already good at climbing by then and simply got in through the windows. The walls of the house started to look in a bit of a state after he began to test out the strength of his super-glue. I became stuck to the kitchen floor one morning and was late for work. I had to put my foot down after that: no more experimenting inside the house.'

Between October 2004 and November 2005, an ambulance was called 17 times to the Metlocks' address. Ian Metlock, Karl's dad, admits that there were times when they thought that Karl's interest was getting out of control. 'It was hard not to get frustrated when we found ourselves in casualty for the second time in a week. The nurses knew us by name.'

Now, three years later, Karl's parents are building a room on the back of their house for their son's collection of over 5000 pieces of Spiderman memorabilia. Instead of growing out of his passion for his hero, Karl aims to make a career out of it by becoming a superhero children's party entertainer.

**Example Question and Answer**

Has Karl's interest in Spiderman made him a happier person?

My response: Yes, Karl's interest in Spiderman has made him happier.

Paraphrase to support my point: Because it says in the text that he used to be lonely and bored. We are told that this all changed when his uncle gave him Spiderman comics.

**1** Has Karl taken his interest in Spiderman too far?

**2** Is Karl's interest in Spiderman making life difficult for those around him?

**3** Should Karl's parents try to stop his interest in Spiderman?

Remember to paraphrase or retell part of the text to back up your answer:

**You could say:**

- I think …

- I think this because …

- In the text we are told …

## Ask yourself

The questions below are about the second paragraph of the article. What are the key words of each question? Would you use a **quotation** or **paraphrase** when answering these questions? Can you explain your choice?

- When was Karl first introduced to Spiderman?
- How did the Spiderman comics change Karl's life?
- How can we tell that Karl felt really excited about the Spiderman comics?
- Do you have a hobby as absorbing as Karl's?

# What's your opinion?

**You are learning:**

How to comment on what a writer's choice of words tells you about how they feel

What's wrong with the way the following opinion is written?

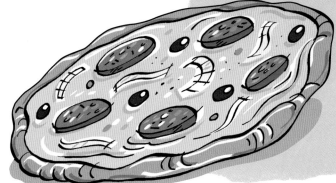

'This pizza tastes disgusting. I'll give it 10/10.'

There is a problem here: 'disgusting' means that the pizza tastes unpleasant but a score of 10/10 suggests that it is the best that can be bought. The word 'disgusting' does not match the score.

Find the problems in the opinions below.

'That film was fantastic: it was the most exciting film I have seen all year. I'll give it 7/10.'

**1** Spot the problem.

SOCCER PRO

3+

'This new computer game is expensive to buy and not very exciting. I'll give it 8/10.'

**2** Explain the problem.

The Beach House Hotel

'The hotel we stayed in was neat and tidy and close to the beach but the beds were uncomfortable. I'll give it 2/10.'

**3** Solve the problem.

### Is it a bird? Is it a plane? No, it's …

# SUPERMAN RETURNS

Based on the words chosen by the reviewer, how many marks out of ten should this film get?

Between 1978 and 1987, four Superman films were made: surely that was enough? Yet here we have the latest Superman film, *Superman Returns*. And it is a good one.

The music hits you from the beginning and lifts you into a fantastic world of excitement. I had a big grin on my face as soon as the music and titles began. The first time you see Superman, the action sequence is absolutely brilliant. I was sitting right on the edge of my seat and feeling very nervous. The way that the camera was used was excellent: I really believed in Superman and I believed that he could fly.

The action scenes were really exciting. I believed in the baddies and I wanted the goodies to win.

My only concern about the film was the love story that threatened to take over. I didn't want to know about Superman's love for Lois Lane. I wanted action! There were a few dreadful kissy scenes where I wanted to stick my fingers down my throat and shout, 'Please – NO!' In the end, though, I was able to forgive the director for the romance. The fast pace and great acting save the day.

## Ask yourself

- Can I explain how the writer feels about the film?
- Can I identify a word in the review which has been carefully chosen by the writer?
- Can I explain what that word shows about the writer's feelings or opinion about the film?
- Can I explain why the writer has chosen to use this word?
- Can I explain how this word makes me feel about seeing this film?

# Using your research skills

## You are learning:

How to retrieve information from several sources

You are a sports journalist working for a local radio station. Your job is to put together reports on local sporting events to be read out during the news bulletin each hour.

| Delete | Reply | Reply All | Forward | Print |

As you know, Langley cricket team played the team from Newley Town today at the Langley ground. Langley lost the match. You will find below three statements taken from various people after the match. Use these to write a short report about the match for tonight's news bulletin.

Thanks,
Jenny

### Tim Powell, ex-player

'All in all, today's match was disappointing. There were flashes of good play, but the team lacked direction. The younger players kept looking to their captain, John Brand, for advice but he didn't seem able to give any clear leadership. I think it is about time that the coach thought about selecting a new captain. John has had a chance; now it is someone else's turn. If this team doesn't start to play well, the spectators will stop coming to watch the matches. We have had a bad run of games this summer.'

### John Brand, team captain

'The match began well with our team batting. The batsmen were calm and sensible, adding runs to the score board fairly quickly. A number of players batted with style and made some excellent shots. By lunchtime, we had built up a good total. I was really pleased with the afternoon's play. The team worked closely together and fielded well. Our bowlers were in good form and we made some good catches. We were unfortunate not to win.'

**Kathy Keene, spectator**

'I'm not sure that this match was worth the ticket price into the cricket ground. Our team lacked energy and, from the start, allowed the visiting team to take control. The only player we can be proud of today was Walling – he batted with spirit and determination, managing to stay in for well over two hours. Really, he held our team together. By lunchtime, though, we were all out for 152 – hardly a brilliant score! After that, things went from bad to worse. Our team seemed to go to sleep – perhaps they ate too much at lunchtime? The captain didn't seem to give them any direction or advice. They just allowed the other team to score too many runs. They didn't deserve to win.'

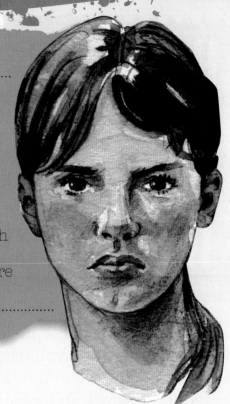

How do these writers **feel** about the cricket match? What is their **opinion**? What is their **viewpoint**?

**1** Read the question carefully and identify the key words.

▼

**2** Briefly remind yourself of each text.

▼

**3** Scan through the texts for key words and useful information.

▼

**4** Decide on an answer by choosing a text.

▼

**5** Paraphrase some information in the text to support your answer.

- Which writer feels happiest about the way that the home team played?
- Which writer is the most unhappy about the way that the home team played?
- Which writer was most pleased with the way that Walling played?
- Which writer is most critical of the team captain?

## Assess your progress

**Writing your match report**

Your match report should be between 75 and 100 words in length. How will you report the match? Will you say that it went well for Langley Town? Will you say that it went badly?

Use the information you have recorded in your research organiser to write the report. You could use the phrases below to help get you started.

- The match began …
- By lunchtime …
- By the end of the day's play …
- Overall …

# Have my reading skills improved?

Successful readers carry a backpack of reading skills. As you read, you should remind yourself of the skills you have in your backpack and select the skill that is most fitting for the task.

making inferences

visualising the text

placing yourself in the shoes of a character

## Ask yourself

- Which of these skills have you improved in?
- Which of these skills do you find the most difficult?
- Why are these skills important?
- When might we use these reading skills?

# Don't be a hero

Her mum, gran and younger brother had disappeared in their beaten-up saloon car into the muddle of twisting Cornish lanes just after breakfast. They were on a trip to Padstow.

'And don't be heroes,' her gran's gravel voice had said from deep inside the car. 'The world has enough dead heroes. You look out for yourselves, hear?' And they'd driven off, due to return around tea-time. A surprising period of freedom stretched ahead. Amy had no idea what to do with it.

Luke was supposed to look after Amy. He was older, stronger. But that holiday he had been strangely jumpy and nervous, especially when Sian was around. Sian and her family were staying two caravans along in a 'Deluxe 1200' with a flat-screen TV and flushing toilet. Luke's eyes were always searching Sian out.

So that day it was no real surprise when Amy found herself trailing behind her brother down to the beach to 'accidentally' bump into Sian. Around Sian stood a group of the friends she had made since she arrived five days earlier. They were trying to organise a party that evening, arguing about where to hold it. No one noticed Luke's arrival. Amy stood a little way off and watched her brother's strange shyness. After five minutes of being ignored, he tried to get the group's attention.

## What's the story?

**Who** are the main characters in the story so far?
**What** are they like?
**What** happens at the beginning of the story?
**Where** is the story taking place?
What can you remember about **when** the story is happening?

# Have my reading skills improved?

Remember: as a successful reader you need to carry an imaginary backpack in which you keep your reading skills. As you read, you should remind yourself of the skills in your backpack and select the skill that is most fitting for the task.

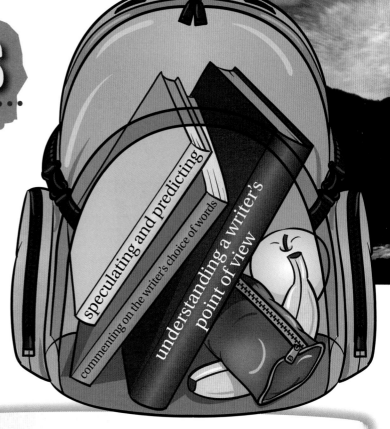

speculating and predicting

commenting on the writer's choice of words

understanding a writer's point of view

'There are sea-caves, you know.' The first time he said it, Luke wasn't heard. Their voices rattled on around him as though he was just another pebble on the beach. Only Amy saw his hunched shoulders and noticed his darting eyes. He tried again: 'Have you heard about the caves?' The tallest boy, with blond hair the colour of sand, turned to face Luke, whose gaze fell immediately. The boy had a look of boredom on his long freckled face.

'So, what are you saying?' demanded the tall boy in a voice that sounded tight. Amy saw her brother's eyes flick to Sian's face and back again to meet the blond boy's gaze.

'Well, my family has been here before – to this holiday beach, I mean … and … and there are sea caves that lead through to another beach that would be really good for a party. I know the way through the caves.' As Luke spoke, his words ran faster, out of control.

'Sea caves. I like that idea.' Sian's voice was picked up and blown by the wind so that Amy could hear the syrup sweetness of her voice.

'Are you sure you know these caves?' The tall boy's arms were folded across his chest and his eyes were hard.

'It might take me a while to remember – but I do know them.' Luke replied quickly.

'Ha! He doesn't know.' The tall boy's laughter set some of the others off grinning.

'I do. I do know them. I do,' Luke begged.

'We'll see, won't we? We'll be outside the shop at six.' Following their leader, the group turned away and clambered up over the sand bank. Their arms were interlocked and their hands rested on each others' shoulders.

Amy watched the group disappear over the sand dune, their voices fading so that only the sound of the waves reached her ears. She turned to an empty space on the sand, her brother already marching away towards the water. She called after him.

'I'm going.' This was all Luke said, his jaw tight.

'But, Mum said –' The promises that she and Luke had made just an hour ago were nagging at Amy's mind.

'I'm going.'

'But, Luke – remember last year. Remember the helicopter and everything. It was on the news. Those people were lucky to escape with their lives, the coastguard said. Remember? Luke!' By now he had reached the mouth of the passage between the cliff and the island. Amy allowed her cupped hands to drop from her mouth and slapped her arms hard against her sides.

'I'm going!' Luke's voice was as hard as the blond boy's had been.

'But, Luke,' Amy's words rasped in her throat as she threw them across the sand, 'THE TIDE!' The water was already creeping over the sand, inch by inch with each new wave. It looked like a calm and soft blanket when you viewed the open sands of the whole bay like this. But in the gully between the steep cliffs and the sides of the island, Amy knew the water would surge and froth, sucking away from the rocks like lips drawing back over jagged teeth.

Amy watched Luke's tanned back as he clambered around the rough edges of the first rock pools. The bones of his spine stretched the skin as he reached down to balance himself over a tricky gully. He is so young, Amy thought. She called to him a final time, her fists clenched at her sides, but he showed no sign of hearing her.

## How does Amy feel as Luke walks away from her towards the sea-caves?

**1** Read the question.

**2** Read a sentence or two from the text.

**3** Choose a reading skill from your backpack which will help you to dig deeper into the text.

**4** Jot down your ideas in response to the question.

# Is my reading improving?

**What's the story?**

**Who** are the main characters in the story so far?
**What** are they like?
**What** happens at the beginning of the story?
**Where** is the story taking place?
What can you remember about **when** the story is happening?

Amy decided that she would give her brother 40 minutes to reappear on the beach. After 40 minutes she was sure that the tide would have covered most of the rock pools. Instead of waiting perhaps she should run to the rescue hut now? She could bang on the door and tell the Australian lifeguards where her brother had gone and they would fetch him back, speeding over the white tops of the waves in their red and yellow rescue boat. But then Amy thought of the crowds that would gather on the beach, enjoying the excitement of a rescue, as they had done in the past. She thought of Sian's face in that crowd, standing on tiptoe to see who had got themselves into trouble this time, the tall blond boy's hands resting on her shoulders. And Amy imagined her brother being

delivered to the safety of the shore, of his burning face and his hunted eyes.

No. She would wait the 40 minutes and then decide what to do. Luke would surely be back by then, anyway.

After an hour, Luke had not returned and Amy made her way reluctantly down the slope of sand towards the gully. The incoming tide was already ankle deep at this point. On the left towered the cliffs and on the right lay the jagged banks of the island. Up ahead, giant fireworks of white froth exploded against the walls. The waves rolled in one after another from the open sea. From the sheltered beach the water always seemed friendly and tame. Here the sea was a beast. Screeching and screaming, white gulls wheeled angrily just a few metres over Amy's head. Everything about this place said, 'DO NOT PASS!'

Amy reached the darkened opening of the cave after a few minutes. It looked smaller than she remembered. She inched along a ledge of rock before squatting at the ragged entrance, her hand resting on the cold, flat surface of the wet rock.

'Lu-uke!' Her voice echoed just as she remembered from last year, sounding hollow and odd. Amy slithered down the tumble of rocks and into the darkness. She used her toes to grip but this meant that she cut the base of her feet on the sharp barnacle shells which covered every surface. The waves pulled at her feet on the slippery rocks, spitting salt high into the air. Her anger blazed. Why was she playing the hero? She should have called the lifeguards instead of trying to play the champion. She thought of Sian, of her styled hair, her fashionable clothes and her winning smile. Was it Sian's fault that Luke was alone somewhere in the caves and that Amy was crouched here with bleeding feet, the water rising with every minute that passed?

'Lu-u-uke!' There was no answer: only the deep boom of the waves crashing against the cliff face.

How does the writer show us that the caves are a dangerous place to be?

1 Read the question carefully, underlining the key words.

2 Read a sentence of the text.

3 Identify words carefully chosen by the writer which fit with the question.

4 Think about what the key word suggests, why the writer has used it and what it helps the reader to understand.

5 Make notes on your ideas.

## Assess your progress

- I can understand what the question is asking me.
- I can choose a reading skill to help me answer the question.
- I can make deductions by linking details in the texts.
- I can choose powerful words from the text and explain what they mean to me.

**Writing a response to the text**

Make a **point** in answer to the question:

- *I think …*

Find some **evidence** from the text to back up your idea:

- *I can tell this when …*
- *The writer has used the word '_____'*

**Explain** what the evidence shows and explain your ideas further:

- *This shows … this suggests …*
- *I think that the character feels …*
- *The writer is trying to …*
- *This helps me to understand …*
- *I think the writer feels …*

**127**